A Student's Guide to College Admissions

ABOUT THE AUTHOR

Harlow G. Unger has taught at two New York–area colleges and counseled high school students on college admissions as a volunteer director of a nonprofit college admissions organization in New York. A graduate of Yale University, with an M.A. from California State University, he is author of four other books on education published by Facts On File: *But What If I Don't Want to Go to College?—A Guide to Successful Careers through Alternative Education; How to Pick a Perfect Private School; "What Did You Learn in School Today?"—A Parent's Guide for Evaluating Your Child's School;* and *Teachers and Educators,* a volume in the American Profiles series. He is now compiling the authoritative Facts On File reference work: *The Encyclopedia of American Education.*

A Student's Guide to College Admissions

Third Edition

Everything Your Guidance Counselor
Has No Time to Tell You

Harlow G. Unger

with
Ronald D. Potier
Director of Admissions
Elizabethtown College

Facts On File®

AN INFOBASE HOLDINGS COMPANY

To My Son
RICHARD

A Student's Guide to College Admissions

Copyright © 1995 by Harlow G. Unger

All rights reserved. No part of this book may be reproduced or utilized in any form or by any means, electronic or mechanical, including photocopying, recording, or by any information storage or retrieval systems, without permission in writing from the publisher. For information contact:

Facts On File, Inc.
460 Park Avenue South
New York NY 10016

Library of Congress Cataloging-in-Publication Data
Unger, Harlow G., 1931–
    A students guide to college admissions : everything your guidance counselor has no time to tell you / Harlow G. Unger. — 3rd ed.
        p.   cm.
    Includes index.
        ISBN 0–8160–3198–3 (alk. paper). — ISBN 0–8160–3199–1 (pbk. :
    alk. paper)
        1. Universities and colleges—United
States—Admission—Handbooks,
    manuals, etc. 2. Universities and colleges—United States—Entrance
requirements—Handbooks, manuals, etc.   I. Title.
    LB2351.2 U55 1995
    378.1'056'0973—dc20   94–42395

Facts On File books are available at special discounts when purchased in bulk quantities for businesses, associations, institutions or sales promotions. Please call our Special Sales Department in New York at 212/683-2244 or 800/322-8755.

Jacket/cover design by Amy Beth Gonzalez

This book is printed on acid-free paper.

Printed in the United States of America

MP FOF 10 9 8 7 6 5 4 3 2 1

CONTENTS

ACKNOWLEDGMENTS

The author wishes to express his deep gratitude to Mr. Ronald D. Potier, former admissions officer at Middlebury College and Clark University and director of admissions at Franklin & Marshall College. He is now director of admissions at Elizabethtown College, Elizabethtown, Pa. Mr. Potier's wisdom and counsel have made this a reference that all college-bound students (and their parents and guidance counselors) can rely on and trust.

Also instrumental in the preparation of this book were Mr. Gordon McK. Bateman, director of financial aid at Elizabethtown College, and Ms. Randy Ladenheim-Gil, editor, Facts On File, Inc.

GETTING STARTED | 1

Getting into the college that's right for you can be a long, complex and frustrating process—especially if the right college is one of America's top-ranked universities. But if you follow all the steps in this guide exactly, I promise you'll succeed.

That may seem like a difficult promise to keep, but it's not, because I won't have to keep it. You will—in the end. You'll have to do the careful planning and studying, and you'll have to get the grades. You'll have to take the Scholastic Assessment Tests (SATs), and you'll have to fill in all the applications neatly and accurately, and write the all-important essays. I can tell you the necessary steps, point you in the right direction, teach you all the little tricks, warn you of the pitfalls, and tell you exactly what the top colleges are looking for. But after I've done all that, you are going to have to do all the work—and you'll have to do it perfectly to succeed.

Naturally, it would help if you happen to have a sparkling personality, are a team captain, editor of your school newspaper or yearbook, and president of your class—and if you also have a grade point average (GPA) of 4.0. But don't worry if you don't have all or even any of those qualities. Most of us don't—which is why, every year, America's highest-ranked colleges accept some students who never even participated in high school sports or extracurricular activities. They also accept some students not ranked in the top 10 percent or even 20 percent of their high school classes—students with averages below 3.0, as well as students with modest SAT scores. In other words, all the best colleges accept some average students and many admit a few below-average students.

"But," you're probably thinking (understandably), "*Barron's* says you need exceptionally high SAT scores to get into the most competitive colleges." Look again. *Barron's* does not really say that. Read a little more carefully, and you'll see that the SAT scores and class rankings listed in *Barron's Profiles of American Colleges* and in most college viewbooks represent *average* or *median* scores and GPAs of matriculated students—not the scores and GPAs of each individual student in those colleges. Remember, median is the middle, which means that only half the student SAT scores for the most selective colleges were above the median. The other half of the SAT scores were *below* the median—many far below that level.

As I said before, some students attending the most selective colleges are below average in many ways. Indeed, such colleges have accepted students who did not even rank in the top 20 percent of their high school classes, let alone the top 10 percent. At Wesleyan University, in Middletown, Connecticut, 11 percent of a recent freshman class of nearly 700 students did not rank in the top 20 percent of their graduating high school classes. Wesleyan is in *Barron's* top category of the 36 most competitive colleges in America.

UNIQUENESS

Obviously, such students must have had other outstanding qualities to earn them admission to such prestigious colleges. But you have such qualities too. We all do, because each of us is unique. There is no other person in the world exactly like you. It's difficult for most of us to recognize what it is that makes each of us unique, because we all tend to want to be like our friends, the people we most admire, and we tend to hide or ignore those characteristics that make us unique or different. Later on, I'll try to show you how to recognize what makes you unique, because, if you want to get into a truly superior college or university, you're going to have to discover and display those qualities. Remember, most top colleges are searching for unique applicants, and, believe it or not, a team captaincy, class presidency and many other high school achievements most of us admire do not necessarily make individuals unique or different. Nor does being a so-called well-rounded student.

There are tens of thousands of well-rounded high school students who dabble in everything in their high school careers and achieve nothing of lasting value for themselves or for others. The most competitive colleges are not looking for well-rounded students. They are looking for unique students who, together, will make up a well-rounded student body. And just as there is a surplus of well-rounded students, there are also many team captains in thousands of schools across the United States— and just as many thousands of class officers—and they don't necessarily have an edge over their classmates when it comes to getting into the most selective colleges.

Where they do have an edge is in getting attention from high school guidance counselors. Almost all college advisers and guidance counselors are dedicated, caring individuals, but they seldom have the time they'd like to give to each of their students. So, they often tend to concentrate on the school's most outstanding college prospects—the so-called stars. It's simply impossible for most guidance counselors to give even 50 students, let alone 100 or 200 or 400, the kind of advice required to help them all get into the colleges of their choice. You'll see why after you've learned how complex the college application process is for just one person—you. Between now and the time you mail your last application, you (and your parents, if they help you) will have to spend several hours a week on the college application process. Multiply the time and effort you spend on yourself by 50 or 100 or more, and you'll understand why guidance counselors and college advisers seldom can give any one student as much undivided attention as he or she may want. And, in most cases, it would be unrealistic of you or your parents to expect that. Remember: The *average* public high school guidance counselor in the U.S. has more than 400 students to advise!

Your college adviser can easily guide you into a two-year community college or a four-year college with an open-enrollment policy that guarantees admission to virtually every applicant. He or she can also probably guide you successfully into a so-called safety school, where your high school record will more than meet the college's entrance requirements.

But most advisers do not have the time to devote to an intensive, 18-month project to help you gain admission to a top-ranked college—a "dream school" or "reach school" whose entrance requirements may, on the surface, seem to rule you out, and, indeed, seem to rule out anyone who is not an athletic, academic or artistic superstar. Nor do most guidance counselors have the time to get to know each of the more than 1,500 colleges and universities intimately enough to know instinctively which ones would be best for each student.

And that's why I've written this book—not to bypass your guidance counselor or college adviser, but to provide you with additional, personalized, in-depth guidance to help you win admittance to the college that's right for you and best for you. I hope the following pages will help qualified students who are not athletic, academic or artistic superstars handle, on their own, the process of applying successfully to a top-ranked college or university. The process may seem complex to you now, but it's actually quite straightforward—long and tedious and filled with hundreds of boring little details, but nevertheless relatively simple for any student and his or her family to handle pretty much by themselves.

Basically, there are three key elements to handling the process: painstaking attention to details; an intimate knowledge of yourself; and an intimate knowledge of six to 10 colleges that will best suit you. It will be your job (and your parents' job if they help you) to handle those details and develop that knowledge. If you rely entirely on your guidance counselor to do the job for you, you may be inviting disappointment.

By all means get all the help you can from your guidance counselor or college adviser. Most guidance counselors do all they possibly can to help in the college admissions process.

They usually write the all-important school recommendations. They arrange for excused absences for students to go on college visits and interviews. They have easy access to forms, catalogs, documents and computer programs, and can save you a lot of time and effort obtaining such things. And they arrange for college representatives to visit your school and talk with students. That kind of help will be very valuable, along with any help you can get from your teachers and other school officials. But remember: Ultimately, the responsibility for getting into college rests with you; and even the most dedicated guidance counselor or college adviser will leave most of the work to you. That's as it should be, because most of the college admissions process and decision making has to be handled by the person who knows you best—you yourself.

I hope this book will show you how to handle that work easily, successfully, and with a minimum of tension and worry. Use the handy timetable and checklist in Appendixes A and B to keep track of all the steps you'll have to take to get into college. Appendix C has some application essays to guide you in handling your correspondence and essay writing. (There's a sample filled-in application in Chapter 4.) Appendix D has a brief explanation of the four standard college entrance exams: PSAT (Preliminary Scholastic Assessment Test), SAT (Scholastic Assessment Tests I and II), and ACT (American College Testing) program. There's also a special note to your parents in Chapter 6 if, as I hope, you and they want to work on the college admissions process as a family team. Most parents are as confused and anxious about the college admissions process as students, and I hope this book will help them too.

Now let's get started getting you into college. And good luck!

HOW TO PICK THE RIGHT 2
COLLEGE—FOR YOU

Anybody can get into college. That I promise you. But not everybody should go. There are, in my opinion, only two good reasons for occupying the much-sought-after seats in a fine college or university: love of learning and preprofessional training.

Although the four years you spend at college will, if you select the right one, be the most wonderful four years of your life, they will also be the most intellectually demanding. College-level work is hard work—and it's work you must do on your own. No one will be there to tell you to do your homework or get busy studying for exams. Fall behind, and you'll flunk out. It's as simple as that. All you'll get from college authorities, in most cases, will be a computer printout telling you you've failed and that you're out.

So, college demands a sense of commitment to self- discipline and hard work, and there's little point going if you don't have a sincere desire to learn or a deep commitment to a particular career goal. If you're only going to college "so I can get a good job," make certain your career choice requires four years of college. Perhaps all you need to succeed is the appropriate technical-school training or two years at a community college, or a good company training program. But don't waste the time and money at a four-year college if you don't have to and really don't want to. College is too long, too hard and too costly to attend simply "because all my friends are going." If you're not sure you want to go to college, you can read my book *But What If I Don't Want to Go to College?*

EARLY PLANNING

If, however, you really want to go—or indeed have to go—to a four-year college, then one way of improving your chances of getting into the college of your choice is to begin planning early, the earlier the better. And it's here that your guidance counselor and parents can and should help you.

Ideally, you and your family should begin making your first tentative college plans no later than the beginning of freshman year in high school, because that's when you begin selecting the high school curriculum that colleges and universities might require and on which they'll judge your application.

Entrance Requirements

It's important to buy a college directory even before beginning high school so you can see what various colleges will require of you during your high school years. There are many directories available at almost any bookstore, but be certain to select a seriously written one rather than one designed to entertain you. Some of the latter are terribly misleading and often contain inaccurate information. For purposes of college selection, I recommend any of the following: *Barron's Profiles of American Colleges*; the College Board's *College Handbook*; Cass and Birnbaum's *Comparative Guide to American Colleges*; or *Peterson's Guide to Four-Year Colleges*. Buy one or two of these guides (more than two is unnecessary and confusing), then study the high school courses each college that interests you requires for admission. Some require three years of math, others four. Some require one, two or three years of science, modern languages, English, history, etc. And almost all the most competitive colleges require honors-level work in these courses and comparably difficult work in elective courses. Elementary-level and nonacademic electives count for little on your record if you plan to aim for the most competitive colleges. So it's a good idea to find out early what high school courses you'll be required to take to gain admission to the type of college that interests you. If you don't, you may shut the door to the college of your choice when you're only 14—and that's not fair to yourself. Also, use your electives to take interesting and challenging courses—for example, astronomy, art or word processing.

If, however, you did make some mistakes in course selection, it probably still is not too late to do something about it—even if you're a high school junior or senior. The first thing to find out is what courses you're lacking to meet the requirements of the college of your choice. Then see if you can make these up by adding them to your regular schedule or by attending summer school—or, if necessary, by repeating a year of high school. That last choice sounds awful but, before you reject it, ask yourself how badly you want to go to the college of your choice. It's usually never too late to decide you want to go there and to do something about it.

But obviously, it's easier if you make the decision as early in your high school career as possible and determine your high school curriculum accordingly.

College Curriculum

Once you decide you want to go to college, the next decision to make is what kind of college to attend, and that should be determined by whether or not you want preprofessional training or are going to seek an education in one or more areas of the arts and sciences. You may not be able to major in journalism or accounting at some liberal arts schools, and an agricultural college could prove a poor choice if you plan on majoring in Renaissance art or literature. In other words, be certain the colleges and universities that you plan to apply to offer a wide selection of courses in areas that most interest you.

If your primary motive for going to college is to study history, literature, biology, or other liberal arts or sciences, then select schools whose professors and departments are renowned in the areas you want to study—schools that attract other students like you, with similar interests. If, on the other hand, your primary motive for going to college is preprofessional training, be certain in advance that the schools of your choice offer *majors* and a *degree* in your particular field of interest.

Of course, there's no reason you can't combine both preprofessional training and studies in the liberal arts and sciences. Many superior colleges offer fine opportunities in both areas. In other words, you can take a wide range of liberal arts and science courses and major in a preprofessional course at the same time.

Still another way to combine study in both areas is to major in arts or sciences as an undergraduate and afterward go to graduate school for professional training.

If you're not sure what you want to get out of college—and many students aren't—the best choices may be colleges that offer a broad range of opportunities. Then you can switch easily from one area to another as you become more certain what area of study most interests you. Remember, a good college or university is like a cafeteria of knowledge, offering an almost endless opportunity for learning about virtually every subject you can imagine—and many that you haven't imagined. College will give you an opportunity to "taste" as many of these subjects as you'd like; and the more subjects you taste, the easier you'll find it to decide what you want to do later on. It's perfectly all right to be undecided and unsure of how you're going to spend the rest of your life, now, when you're 16, 17 or 18. When you're 35, you'd better have made up your mind. But few of us know what we want to do with our lives when we're still in our teens, and it's unfair of others to try to force you to make up your mind now. Your college years will help you make such choices.

The Liberal Arts

Many students and their parents wonder about the "value" of a liberal arts education. "What kind of job can I get as an English, history or philosophy major?" is a question that's asked all the time, because so many entry- level jobs in business require skills that are not learned in English literature classes.

The answer is complex. Here's what the University of Michigan says about the value of a liberal arts education:

> For more than two thousand years, our civilization has valued the idea of a liberal [arts] education. The assumption behind this idea is that knowledge and the search for knowledge are in themselves humanizing: that the exploration of the unknown

> both engages and reflects upon the exploring self. The end of a liberal education is the creation of knowledgeable, wise, just,and happy men and women, prepared to live productively and meaningfully in society. To achieve such an education, students must learn to analyze, classify, and evaluate the experiences which life offers; then they must learn to use these faculties both to develop the values and principles by which they will live and to master the knowledge, skills, and techniques appropriate to their most particular ambitions.

What that great university is saying is that the liberal arts and sciences are the story of our—of your—society, your country, your world, your entire civilization and culture, and how they developed. The study of the liberal arts and sciences teaches free people how to remain free—how to lead and govern themselves, how to pursue truth and wisdom, and, above all, how to learn. Once you have learned how to learn, you'll find it easy to pick up any skill you need for any particular job later on—either in graduate school or on the job itself. Virtually every major corporation, postgraduate professional school and government agency recognizes the value of a liberal arts or science degree; and those with such degrees are now in great demand.

CHOOSING A COLLEGE ENVIRONMENT

In addition to the academic decisions (preprofessional, liberal arts, etc.) you must make in selecting your list of colleges, another decision that's important to make is environmental. College will be your *home* as well as your *place of work* for four years. To succeed in your work, it's important that you live in a comfortable environment. You must decide whether you want to live in a large college community or a small one; in the city, suburbs or country; in a coed or single-sex college; in a religiously, ethnically or racially oriented school, or in a secular college; in a state-run or private college; far from home or near—or even at home, where you can attend a "commuter" college; in a single room or with roommates; on campus or off; in dormitories or apartments. Crime rates are another important consideration.

All these environmental factors will affect your life for the next four years in every way—socially, academically, emotionally and even physically. For different individuals there are advantages and disadvantages to every collegiate environment. A large college will give you far less chance than a small one to know your teachers and college administrators. You could find yourself socially isolated unless you're able to reach out aggressively to make friends and participate in extracurricular activities.

A small college, where everyone gets to know everyone else, can prove stifling for some students while providing warmth and comfort for others. City colleges offer a wide range of cultural opportunities—but far more danger of crime, both on and off campus. Off-campus living quarters incur housekeeping responsibilities and can isolate you from on-campus activities. But dormitories can be noisy and can interfere with your work and sleep. Living at home and commuting to college will mean big financial savings, but could mean missing much of the social and extracurricular activities that make the college experience unique.

Coeducational institutions provide a more conventional male-female social environment that makes dating easier, but can prove distracting for many students—even embarrassing for some, who simply do not want to share personal living quarters with members of the opposite sex. And that's all right. The point is, you must choose the environment that you believe is right for *you*—not what others say is right for you. For many students, a single-sex college offers a far better environment for the serious pursuit of learning during the week—with plenty of time for socializing at nearby colleges on weekends.

There are more than five dozen all-women's or predominantly women's colleges in the United States, several of which are among the most selective, prestigious colleges in the country. Statistics show that women's colleges accelerate the movement of women into traditionally "male" fields such as science, politics or business.

The U.S. Department of Education found that women attending women's colleges are three times as likely to earn bachelor's degrees in economics as those at coeducational colleges, and 1.5 times as likely to major in science and mathematics. That's important in after-college life, according to the department, which tracked more than 12,000 men and women from high school until they were 32. That study showed that women with four years of college only matched the average earnings of men with *high school diplomas*, while women who took more than two college-level mathematics courses achieved pay equity with men.

The sad truth is that, despite laws banning gender discrimination in education, the largest coeducational universities remain male-dominated in many, many subtle ways, with huge stadiums and arenas for hundreds of thousands of paying spectators who are probably there to cheer men, not women. Most of the women who are televised at such events are scantily clad cheerleaders—again, cheering for men, not women.

Academically, women at coeducational institutions fare no better. They tend to shy away from science, mathematics and engineering and enroll in such academic areas as literature, music and art—the traditional "ornamental arts" that women were forced to study in the 19th century to prepare for lives as "ornaments" in their future husbands' homes.

In contrast, 80 percent of students at women's colleges take four years of science and mathematics, compared to only two years in coeducational colleges. Graduates of women's colleges also score higher than *women* graduates of coeducational colleges on graduate school admissions tests. They also attend graduate school more frequently, and they earn more doctorates. Indeed, graduates of just five women's colleges—Barnard, Bryn Mawr, Mount Holyoke, Smith and Wellesley—account for 43 percent of the math doctorates and 50 percent of the engineering doctorates earned by American women.

All-told, women's colleges represent less than 5 percent of all American colleges, but account for one-third of the female board members of Fortune 1,000 companies and equally disproportionately high percentages of women entering professional fields such as medicine, law, science and engineering.

There are many reasons for the success of women's colleges. One is that the many successful *female* professors there provide inspiring role models often unavailable to women at coeducational colleges, where male-dominated faculties, consciously or unconsciously, sometimes tend to take women students less seriously than men.

Women's colleges, in contrast, provide a supportive environment and unlimited opportunities for women to exercise academic and social leadership that all but the most talented might be denied at coeducational institutions. And finally, women's colleges have none of the classroom and campus social distractions of a coeducational environment, thus allowing students to concentrate on their work.

Another college-selection factor to consider, depending on its importance to you, is whether you want to attend a religiously affiliated or an ethnically or racially oriented school. These are personal choices you alone can make. Every secular college has organizations and adequate facilities for every student to associate with people of similar interests and religious beliefs, and ample on-campus and off-campus places of worship. And such secular schools also offer a wide variety of courses dealing with religious and cultural history of all kinds. Parochial and ethnically or racially oriented schools, on the other hand, usually offer far more specialized courses related to the particular group of students attending those schools. Moreover, the student body will be far more homogeneous, and you'll probably meet fewer students who are different from you and hold different ideas, beliefs and opinions; and that might prove less stimulating intellectually.

Distance from home is another important consideration. Many high school students sincerely believe they'd be happier a million miles from home and parents—until they get there. Other students feel they cannot bear to leave their family and friends at home, and they miss out on the college experience by attending a commuter school and returning home after classes each day—just as they did at high school.

One mistake to avoid in selecting a college environment is to pick a school simply because some or many of your high school friends will be going there. It's sad to part with old friends, but you must pick your college on the basis of what's best for *your* future, not theirs.

Another environmental consideration is the extent of the college's extracurricular activities. Many schools have their own radio and television stations, owned and operated by students, along with daily newspapers; literary, scientific and humor magazines; a variety of yearbooks; complete professional theater facilities for student drama societies; ballet troupes; glee clubs, choruses, orchestras and bands that not only perform on campus but travel around the country and sometimes the world during vacations to perform elsewhere. Some schools have varsity sports only; others offer a wide variety of sports at both the varsity and intramural levels. It's best to make a list of all the activities you feel you'll need to make your four-year college life fulfilling and joyful, and then pick accordingly.

Still another environmental factor you must consider, unfortunately, is the on-campus and off-campus crime rate. Federal law requires all colleges and universities to publish and make readily available their security and crime-reporting policies and publicize the number of on-campus killings, assaults, sexual assaults, robberies, burglaries and other crimes. It's important that you find out these figures before you consider applying to a college. There's some crime everywhere, of course—even on the most beautiful rural campuses. Not every student who goes to college is a well-adjusted person. For the kind of money you'll have to spend to go to college, you have a right not to have to live in fear. So find out the security precautions and crime rates before applying, recognizing, of course, that big-city colleges will probably have higher crime rates than rural schools, but offer cultural advantages that rural schools do not. Everything, in other words, is a trade-off.

And finally, don't forget to take into consideration the cultural environment of each college. It's true that you'll be spending most of your time working—as everyone in the adult world does. But you also need to relax and play if you're going to do your best at work. So be sure to ask about and look into the recreational opportunities—concerts, theater, movies, sports and other nonorganized activities—that are important to you.

All of this may seem confusing, but it's really not. Let's look back for a moment. So far, here are the decisions you've had to make in drawing up a list of colleges that you may want to apply to:

1. Whether you really want to go to college in the first place
2. Why you want to go—for preprofessional training, interest in the liberal arts and sciences, or both

3. The environment that you'll need to make college a nice place in which to live as well as work

Level of College Difficulty

Before making those three decisions, let's discuss one more preapplication decision you'll have to make—namely, the degree of academic commitment you are willing to make during your four years at college.

Remember that most of the same books are available in almost every college library throughout the country. The knowledge is there for any motivated student to obtain and absorb. In other words, you can get almost the same education and achieve the same measure of success regardless of which college or university you attend. It's true that many brilliant and successful people graduate from Yale, Harvard, Princeton and Stanford universities, but equally gifted students also graduate from less-known schools such as City College in New York, Whittier College in California or Eureka College in Illinois, to mention just a few. What, then, is the difference between various categories of colleges and universities?

The answer is the difficulty of entrance; the renown of the faculty; the funds and facilities available for education, recreation and living quarters; and the degree of academic commitment demanded of each student and faculty member. The vast majority of the more than 1,500 four-year degree-granting colleges in the United States operate on near or complete open enrollment—i.e., they accept nearly 100 percent of all applicants. There are more than 1,200 colleges that operate in this fashion, accepting students almost on a first-come, first-served basis but giving preference to students from the immediate geographic area. The vast majority of publicly operated state colleges and universities fall into this category.

A recent *Barron's* listed only about 130 American colleges that accept fewer than half their applicants. Only 88 (e.g., Colgate, Emory, Grinnell, Lehigh, Oberlin, Reed, Smith, Villanova, etc.) fell into the "Highly Competitive" category. These colleges generally accepted between one-third and one-half of their applicants. A mere 45 colleges (Amherst, Bowdoin,

Brown, Duke, Harvard, Princeton, Stanford, Williams, Yale, etc.) were ranked in the prestigious "Most Competitive" category—i.e., colleges that accepted fewer than one-third of their applicants and often less than 20 percent.

The figure 45 is misleading, however, because the category included two specialized colleges; four service academies, to which applicants must be nominated; and two engineering schools, such as Massachusetts Institute of Technology, open only to a relatively few students with special talents and qualifications. Thus, there were only 37 liberal arts colleges in this last category, and many of them received 10 or more applications for every opening. All but seven are private colleges, with costs of tuition, room and board approaching $30,000 a year.

Of the 88 colleges in the second-ranked category of "Highly Competitive" schools, 12 were specialized schools open to relatively few qualified students. That left only 64 liberal arts colleges in this category open to most students; and, again, there were many, many more applicants than there were available seats. Of this group, the vast majority were costly private colleges, with total annual costs of attending in the $20,000-to-$30,000 range.

But don't let these statistics discourage you. Although there are indeed far more applicants than available seats at the most selective colleges, many of the applicants have no business applying to such colleges—as you'll see when you read some of the application essays in Appendix C of this book. So, if you believe you're a good candidate for a top college, by all means apply. Remember, every college in America is competing with every other college to attract the most desirable students. I hope that means you.

Remember, too, that the ease or difficulty of admission does not necessarily reflect the ease or difficulty of the academic work at college. Indeed, the only thing difficult about many of the most selective colleges is getting in, not staying in or doing the academic work. Most of the undergraduate academic work at Yale University, for example, is the same as that at almost every other accredited college in the United States—no easier or harder. As most students will attest, it's easy to "breeze" through Yale or Harvard or any other highly selective college—and you can too!

Until recently, 80 percent of undergraduates at Princeton and 92 percent of students at Stanford got nothing but A's and B's. At some of the most selective colleges, half the students graduate with honors and few, if any, ever flunk out. Stanford long ago eliminated the F and only recently instituted a grade of NC, for "no credit." The NC is for internal purposes only and does not appear on a student's transcript.

Some college officials claim "grade inflation" is the result of selective admissions policies that admit only the brightest, honors students to enroll. But the truth is that grade inflation lets many students at selective colleges get high grades without much effort. A survey of 3,000 Ivy League students found that 44 percent didn't know the name of the Speaker of the U.S. House of Representatives, 59 percent couldn't name four U.S. Supreme Court justices and 35 percent couldn't identify the British prime minister.

Grade inflation began in the 1960s, when sympathetic teachers started giving automatic passing grades to permit students to remain in college and preserve their student exemptions from the military draft that would have sent them to fight in the Vietnam War. It remained a habit long after the war ended.

So, if your high school work has been good enough to get you into a selective college, you probably won't have any trouble doing the work there. If you're qualified, by all means apply.

But surely, you may be asking, there must be some differences between the most selective and less selective colleges other than the difficulty of admissions. The answer is yes—a few, but not many. For one thing the most selective colleges usually have more money than less selective schools and can afford to hire some of the world's most famous professors, including Nobel Prize winners. That's certainly a plus—*if* you happen to be one of the few, lucky students who get a chance to study under those professors.

The probability is you will not get that chance, however, because many only teach graduate school students. Those who teach undergraduates usually see their classes oversubscribed. In any case, few, if any, such famed professors will actually "teach" you on a one-to-one basis. They're too busy doing research and writing books to do anything but lecture in huge lecture halls. Chances are you'll gain far more knowledge from a lesser-known professor who has time to get to know you and teach you in a small class.

Another, more important difference between some selective colleges and their less selective counterparts is the breadth of course choices in each department. The most selective colleges usually have more funds to offer more courses, and if you're particularly interested in studying one subject in great depth, you'd be wise to be certain the colleges you apply to have enough course offerings to satisfy your needs.

There may be many other differences between some less selective colleges and their better-known, highly selective counterparts. One such difference may be the wealth of various colleges and that, in turn, may affect the size of their libraries and the number of laboratories and other specialized facilities and how well equipped such facilities may be. Another difference may be the size and number of facilities for extracurricular activities and sports. These are all factors you should explore and consider in selecting colleges to apply to.

Still another difference between selective and less selective schools is the "name." A "name school," such as Harvard, Yale, Stanford and others, often "looks" better on a resume to some prospective employers, and that can sometimes make it easier to get a job after graduation and, perhaps, a higher starting salary. Many employers, often unfairly, favor job applicants who graduated from the same colleges as they.

You'd be foolish, however, to spend upwards of $100,000 attending any four-year college if your only reason for going there is its name. You'd be far better off—and probably get a better education—going to a college that's truly "good" for you and then, later on, if you still want that "name" on your resume, go ahead and get a master's degree from a name college. It will look just as good on your resume, I promise.

WHAT'S A "GOOD" SCHOOL?

In simplest terms, a "good" school is one that's good for you, one that will challenge you to function at your very best. Virtually every accredited American college and university is a good school, but not every one is good for you. The only way to decide is through careful research. First, study some independently written college selection aids. Second, write for materials from the colleges themselves. Third, visit the colleges that interest you the most, so that you can see for yourself whether you want to go there.

Independent College Selection Aids

There are many college selection aids on the market, but you'll really only need one or two. You can buy more, of course, but in the end you'll find yourself more confused—and far poorer. I strongly advise against buying the more entertaining, subjective guides that go into things such as the party life of the school and student personalities. Most are the opinions of a few students and are usually inaccurate. Even when accurate one year, they become inaccurate the next and probably won't be true by the time you get to college.

So, stick to the serious—and accurate—books listed earlier in this chapter (*Barron's*, the College Board's *College Handbook*, Cass and Birnbaum, and *Peterson's*) or one of the computerized programs that you can either buy in software shops or, perhaps, find in your high school guidance office.

Perhaps the most useful—and certainly the most accurate— selection aid is the *College Admissions Data Handbook*, which contains "profiles" (Figure 1) of more than 1,000 four-year colleges. Unfortunately, Wintergreen Orchard House Inc. (P.O. Box 15899, New Orleans, LA 70175-5899; tel. 1-800-321-9479), which publishes the *Handbook*, does not sell individual profiles, and the entire *Handbook* is not only expensive—in the hundreds of dollars—it's far more information than you'll ever need. So the best thing for you to do is go to the public library or to your guidance counselor's office and look at (and photocopy) the college profiles that interest you.

Wintergreen Orchard House also has a CD-ROM program that may be in the office of your college adviser or guidance counselor. Called *Keys to College*, the program includes all the college profiles from the entire *College Admissions Data Handbook*, an index of majors and sports, a database of more than 2,500 private scholarships, and a college-search program that identifies 20 to 50 best college "fits" for you, if you punch in all the characteristics you want your college to have. Again, it's needlessly expensive ($499) for you to buy. Try to access it in your guidance office or a public library.

Another useful guide is *The College Handbook*, which is published by the College Entrance Examination Board. It also provides college profiles, and it is available in most major bookstores and public libraries, and from the College Board

(45 Columbus Avenue, New York, NY 10023; tel.: 1-212-713-8000). It's a bit less complete than the *College Admissions Data Handbook*, but it's a good substitute if you can't obtain the other.

In addition to the program mentioned above from Wintergreen Orchard House, there are many other computer software programs now available in your school guidance office or via modem. Guidance Information Services puts out one of the best computer programs available to guidance offices. Also available in many guidance offices is the College Board's computer search service that, like the Wintergreen Orchard House program, allows quick retrieval of college descriptions on the basis of such data as college size, location and other factors essential in your search for colleges.

There are a number of CD-ROM programs that allow you to call up complete college-course catalogs and profiles and institute your own search by punching in the characteristics you most want from your future college and letting the program call up the list of schools that fit that description. Such programs are available for sale through software shops, but they're fairly costly and only a few are truly accurate. I strongly advise your limiting your purchases to one of the printed directories I mentioned and tapping into software at your high school guidance office or via a modem, if you have that capability.

Use the selection aids discussed above to narrow your list of college choices as much as possible by carefully comparing the characteristics of each college with the characteristics most important for you. Make a checklist with all the characteristics you'd like your personal dream school to have. You can then either use computer software to identify such schools or simply use a sheet of paper, with the characteristics listed on the left, opposite columns for each of the colleges you're considering. You can put a check opposite each characteristic under the names of each college with that advantage.

Descriptive Materials from Colleges

College directories and software only list the available facts about each college. They are seldom able to give you a realistic picture of what life at each college is like. For that information, write to each college admissions office (their addresses are all listed in the various selection aids mentioned above) for "viewbooks," which are descriptive brochures with pictures and information about each college. Most colleges also have videos that they'll lend you or your guidance counselor. You may also want to ask for a course catalog and for brochures on specific courses, sports or extracurricular activities that are of particular interest to you. Many viewbooks contain listings of courses offered at the particular college, but course catalogs offer more detailed descriptions of each course in every department. Ask, too, for financial aid information if you want; and be certain to ask each college for a copy of its own profile of the most recent freshman class, with the characteristics of its applicants and of its current freshman class—i.e., the applicants it accepted and who enrolled. Most colleges now publish all or part of their profiles in their viewbooks, but it's best to ask for one anyway when writing for information from each college. Remember, though, you'll find the most complete and objective profiles in the *College Admissions Data Handbook* (see Figure 1).

Eventually, of course, college applicants will be able to get all such information interactively, via modem on their home computers, from services such as the College Board. By simply punching in the name of the university that interests you, you'll be able to get full information on any department or activity at the university, along with all details for applying, obtaining financial aid and enrolling. A voice will welcome you to the university, take you on a guided tour, allow you to stop in any department and even apply for admission. You'll also be able to conduct "searches" on your computer for colleges that can fulfill your special needs and interests. Thus, you'd be able to punch "nuclear physics" into your computer and have it search for and produce a list of colleges that offer undergraduate programs in that subject.

UNSOLICITED MATERIALS

In addition to the materials you request from colleges, you'll also receive a large amount of unsolicited materials from colleges that want you to consider them on your list. These colleges obtained your name by purchasing computerized lists of high school students who take the PSATs or SATs in their junior

Michigan, University of, Ann Arbor

University of Michigan – Ann Arbor

Main telephone: 313 764-1817
President: James J. Duderstadt, Ph.D.
Director of Admissions: Theodore Spencer, M.S.
Admissions telephone: 313 764-7433
Director of Financial Aid: Harvey Grotrian, M.A.
Financial aid telephone: 313 763-6600
Public university established in 1817, became coed in 1871.

515 Jefferson
Ann Arbor, Michigan 48104-2210
Full-time undergraduates: 11,637 Men, 10,408 Women.
Part-time undergraduates: 682 Men, 657 Women.
Graduate enrollment: 7,887 Men, 5,574 Women.
Total enrollment: 36,845.
SAT and FAF #1839, ACT and FFS #2062.

ADMISSIONS

Requirements

Graduation from secondary school is required; GED is accepted. 20 units and the following program of study are recommended: 4 units of English, 4 units of mathematics, 3 units of science, 4 units of foreign language, 3 units of social studies, 1 unit of history. English units should include at least two rigorous writing courses. Some qualified in-state applicants admitted before receipt of test scores. In-state applicants from unaccredited schools may be asked to take additional exam before being considered. Higher GPA and test scores required of out-of-state applicants. Portfolio required of art program applicants. Audition required of music program applicants. 3-4 units of math and 2 units of laboratory science including chemistry required of nursing program applicants. 4 units of math and at least 1 unit each of chemistry and physics required of engineering program applicants. 4 units of foreign language recommended of literature, science, and arts program applicants. Comprehensive Studies Program and Summer Bridge Program for applicants not normally admissible. SAT or ACT required. TOEFL or MELAB and SAT or ACT required of foreign applicants. Campus visit recommended. Off-campus interviews not available. Admission may be deferred for one year. Application fee $40, not refundable.

Basis for Candidate Selection

Academic: Secondary school record, standardized test scores, school's recommendation, class rank, and essay.

Other: Particular talent or ability is emphasized. Extracurricular participation, geographical distribution, and alumni/ae relationship are considered.

Admissions Procedure

Normal sequence: Take SAT or ACT by February 1 of 12th year. Application deadline is February 1. Notification of admission on rolling basis. Reply is required by May 1. $200 tuition deposit, nonrefundable. 4% of freshmen enter in terms other than fall.

Special programs: Early entrance/early admission program.

Transfers: Transfer students accepted for terms other than fall. In fall 1993, 15% of all new students were transfers into all classes. 2,224 transfer applications were received, 1,140 were accepted. Application deadline is February 1 for fall; November 1 for spring. Minimum 2.5 GPA required. Lowest course grade accepted is "C." Maximum number of transferable semester hours is 60. At least 60 semester hours must be completed at the university to receive degree.

Learning Disabled Students: Essay required. Untimed tests are accepted. Foreign language requirements may be substituted. Lighter course load and additional time to complete degree permitted.

Advanced Placement/CLEP: Credit and placement may be granted through CEEB Advanced Placement exams for scores of 3 or higher. Credit and placement may be granted through CLEP subject exams, ACT PEP exams, and challenge exams.

Freshman Class Profile

In fall 1993, 68% of 19,152 applicants were offered admission. 38% of those accepted matriculated. Size of freshman class: 4,893; 80% from public schools.

84% of accepted applicants took SAT; 59% took ACT.

Student Body Characteristics

30% are from out of state. 2% are from foreign countries. Average age of undergraduates is 20.

Composition of student body:

Asian-American	10.0
Black	8.0
Hispanic	5.0
White	73.0
Other	4.0
	100.0%

FINANCIAL

Expenses

Tuition (1994-95): $4,894 per year (in-state freshmen and sophomores); $5,376 (in-state juniors and seniors); $15,222 (out-of-state freshmen and sophomores), $16,301 (out-of-state juniors and seniors). Room & Board: $4,659. Books (school's estimate): $635.

Financial Aid

FAFSA: Priority filing date is March 15; deadline is September 30. Income tax forms: Priority filing date is April 15; deadline is September 30. Notification of awards begins March 15. In 1993-94, aid was granted to 35% of all undergraduates; 43% of freshmen who applied for aid. 90% of aid is need-based.

Scholarships and Grants

Pell grants, SEOG, state scholarships and grants, college/university scholarships and grants, private scholarships and grants, ROTC scholarships, academic merit scholarships, and athletic scholarships. In 1993-94, aid ranged from $200 to $12,500. 30% of all undergraduates received aid in the form of scholarships and grants. 50% of undergraduates who applied for aid received scholarships and grants. A total of $34,000,000 in scholarships and grants was awarded to undergraduate aid applicants. Average amount of scholarships and grants awarded freshmen: $4,600. 40% of all enrolled freshmen received scholarships and grants.

Loans

Perkins, PLUS, Stafford, NSL, Health Professions Loans, state loans, college/university loans, private loans, SLS, and unsubsidized Stafford loans. Installment plan. In 1993-94, loans ranged from $25 to $14,000. 32% of all undergraduates received loans. 80% of undergraduates who applied for aid received loans. A total of $23,500,000 in loans was awarded to undergraduate aid applicants. Average amount of loans awarded freshmen: $2,000. 35% of all enrolled freshmen received loans.

Student Employment

40% of full-time undergraduates work on campus during school year. College Work/Study Program. Institutional employment. Students may expect to earn an average of $1,200 during school year. Off-campus part-time employment opportunities rated "excellent."

ACADEMIC

Accreditation

Accredited by NCACS; numerous professional accreditations.

Faculty

Instructional staff: 2,713 full-time; 621 part-time.

Doctorates	90%	Masters	8%
Bachelors	2%		

Student-Faculty ratio: 11 to 1.

Curriculum

Baccalaureate degrees offered: A.B., B.A.Ed., B.Bus.Admin., B.F.A., B.Gen.Studies, B.Mus., B.Mus.Arts, B.S., B.S.Chem., B.S.Dent.Hyg., B.S.Ed., B.S.Eng., B.S.Med.Chem., B.S.Nat.Res., B.S.Nurs., B.S.Pharm.

Figure 1 *A profile* of the University of Michigan, Ann Arbor, Mich., from the College Admissions Data Handbook. Compiled from data provided by college admissions offices, the CADH contains profiles of more than 1,500 four-year, degree-granting colleges across America. Profiles such as this are indispensable aids in*

– University of Michigan – Ann Arbor (MI) –

Majors

College of Engineering: Aerospace, Atmospheric/Oceanic Science, Atmospheric/Oceanic/Space Sciences, Chemical, Civil/Environmental, Computer, Electrical, Engineering, Engineering Physics, Engineering Science, Industrial/Operations, Materials/Metallurgical, Materials Science/Engineering, Mechanical, Naval Architecture/Marine, Nuclear. *College of Literature, Science, and the Arts:* Afro-American/African Studies, American Culture, Ancient/Biblical Studies, Anthropology, Anthropology/Zoology, Applied Mathematics, Arabic Studies, Arts/Ideas, Asian Studies, Astronomy, Biological Sciences, Biology, Biomedical Sciences, Biophysics, Botany, Cellular/Molecular Biology, Chemistry, Chinese, Classical Archaeology, Classical Studies, Communication, Comparative Literature, Computer Science, Creative Writing, Economics, Engineering, English, Film/Video Studies, French, General Biology, General Studies, Geological Science, German, Greek, Hebrew, History, History of Art, Humanities, Individualized Concentration, International Studies, Iranian, Islamic Studies, Italian, Japanese, Journalism, Judaic Studies, Latin, Latin American/Caribbean Studies, Latino/Hispanic-American Studies, Linguistics, Literature, Mathematics, Medieval/Renaissance Collegium, Meteorology, Microbiology, Middle East/North Africa Area Studies, Music, Near Eastern/North African Studies, Near Eastern Studies, Oceanography, Philosophy, Physics, Political Science, Psychology, Psychology/Science, Religion, Romance Linguistics, Russian, Russian/East European Studies, Scandinavian Studies, Slavic Languages/Literatures, Social Anthropology, Social Science, Sociology, Spanish, Speech, Statistics, Theatre/Drama, Turkish, Western European Studies, Women's Studies, Zoology. *Division of Kinesiology:* Kinesiology, Movement Science, Sports Management/Communication, Teacher Education. *School of Art:* Ceramics, Computer Graphics, Design, Drawing, Graphic Design, Industrial Design, Interior Design, Metal Work/Jewelry Design, Painting, Photography, Printmaking, Sculpture, Weaving/Textile Design. *School of Business Administration:* Accounting, Business Administration, Finance, Human Resources, Marketing. *School of Dentistry:* Dental Hygiene. *School of Education:* Art, Elementary, Music, Secondary, Special. *School of Music:* Bassoon, Carillon, Cello, Clarinet, Composition, Dance, Double Bass, Drama, Euphonium, Flute, French Horn, Harp, Harpsichord, Jazz Studies, Music, Music Education, Music History, Music Technology, Music/Technology, Music Theory, Musical Theater, Oboe, Organ, Percussion, Performance, Piano, Saxophone, String Instruments, Theater, Trombone, Trumpet, Tuba, Viola, Violin, Voice, Wind Instruments. *School of Natural Resources:* Engineering, Environmental Advocacy, Environmental Communications, Environmental Instruction, Environmental Policy/Behavior, Environmental Science, Field Biology, Forestry, Landscape Design/Planning, Natural Resources, Natural Resources/Biometry, Natural Resources/Biophysics, Natural Resources/Sociobehavioral Science, Outdoor Recreation, Resource Ecology/Management, Wildlife. *School of Nursing:* Nursing.

Academic Overview

Students in Coll of Literature, Science, and the Arts may elect courses in other colleges. 10% of freshmen invited to participate in four-year Honors Program. Unified Sciences Honors Program for freshmen and sophomores includes departmental honors programs and courses. Cooperative program in natural resources. Journalism certificate. Residential College (subdivision of Coll of Literature, Science, and the Arts) offers four-year curriculum in residential quarters with small classes and emphasis on independent study and an innovative environment. General education requirement. Self-designed majors. Double majors. Dual degrees. Independent study. Accelerated study. Honors program. Phi Beta Kappa. Pass/fail grading option. Internships. Cooperative education program in engineering. Teacher certification in early childhood, elementary, and secondary education and in 32 specific subject areas. Graduate school at which qualified undergraduates may take graduate-level classes. Preprofessional programs in law, medicine, pharmacy, dentistry, architecture, and business administration. 2-2 program with Sch of Business Administration. 3-2 engineering and natural resources programs. Inter-university programs in architecture, engineering, forestry, health sciences, and natural resources. Combined bachelor's/graduate degree programs include D.D.S., M.A.Journ., M.Arch., M.D., and M.Pub.Pol. Member of Committee on Institutional Cooperation. Washington Semester. Exchange programs with Big 10 institutions and U of Chicago. Exchange programs abroad in Germany (U of Tubingen), England (Cambridge U), and Sweden (U of Uppsala). Study abroad also in many countries. Education specialist certificate offered. Museums of anthropology, archaeology, art, natural sci-

ence, paleontology, and zoology, audio-visual center, planetarium, electron microscope, biology station, geology camp, athletic campus, medical center, nuclear lab, botanical garden, herbarium, arboretum. Library of 6,527,636 volumes, 70,693 periodicals, and 4,905,227 microforms. 26 libraries on campus. 3,500 IBM/IBM-compatible, Apple/Macintosh, and RISC-/UNIX-based microcomputers; all are networked. Client/LAN operating systems include Apple/Macintosh, DOS, OS/2, UNIX/XENIX/AIX, Windows NT, X-windows, Banyan, LocalTalk/AppleTalk, Novell. Students may access Digital, Hewlett-Packard, IBM, Sun, and UNISYS minicomputer/mainframe systems, BITNET, Internet. Residence halls may be equipped with networked microcomputers. Computer facilities are available to all students. Hours: 24 hours. Numerous computer languages and software packages available. AFROTC, NROTC, and ROTC on campus.

Academic Experience

95% of freshmen return for their sophomore year. Average GPA of freshmen after first year is 2.9 on a 4.0 scale. 62% of freshmen graduate after four years. The most popular majors in 1993 were psychology, engineering, and biology.

Guidance Facilities/Student Services

Remedial learning services. Nonremedial tutoring. Placement service. Health service. Women's center. Day care. Minority student, military, veteran student, older student, birth control, career, personal, academic, psychological, and religious counseling. Sexual Assault Prevention/Awareness Center, Lesbian and Gay Male Program Office, Alcohol and Other Drug Abuse. Learning disabled student services. Handicapped student services. Most of campus is accessible to the physically handicapped.

EXTRACURRICULAR ACTIVITIES

Athletics

Intercollegiate baseball, basketball, cross-country, diving, football, golf, gymnastics, ice hockey, swimming, tennis, track and field (indoor), track and field (outdoor), wrestling for men. Intercollegiate basketball, cross-country, diving, field hockey, golf, gymnastics, softball, swimming, tennis, track and field (indoor), track and field (outdoor), volleyball for women. Numerous club and intramural sports. 2% of students participate in intercollegiate sports. 90% of students participate in intramural sports. Member of Big 10 Conference, Central Collegiate Hockey Association, Midwest Field Hockey Conference, NCAA Division I, NCAA Division I-A for football.

Social Organizations

43 fraternities, 36 chapter houses; 24 sororities, 18 chapter houses. 25% of men join a fraternity and 25% of women join a sorority.

Other Student Activities

Student government, newspaper (Michigan Daily), literary magazine, yearbook, radio station, television station. 25 honor societies. Numerous religious groups. Several minority groups. Numerous foreign student groups. Musical, drama, and literary groups. A total of 522 registered organizations.

REGULATIONS

Housing

Students may live on or off campus. Coed, women's, men's dormitories; sorority, fraternity, on-campus married-student housing. Cooperatives, special housing for handicapped students. 31% of students live on campus.

Automobiles

All students may have cars on campus.

Other

Alcohol permitted on campus for students of legal age; additional restrictions apply. Class attendance policies set by individual instructors. Honor code. Hazing prohibited.

GENERAL

Environment/Transportation

2,665-acre, suburban campus in Ann Arbor (population: 109,592), 50 miles west of Detroit. Served by bus and train; major airport serves Detroit. School operates campus transportation system. Public transportation serves campus.

Calendar

Semester system; classes begin in mid-September and early January. Two summer sessions of seven weeks each; one spring-summer term of 14 weeks. Orientation for new students held in June, July, August, September, and January.

narrowing your list of colleges to the six or eight to which you'll eventually apply. University of Michigan is ranked in Barron's second-highest category of "Highly competitive" colleges and universities. (*Copyright 1994, Wintergreen Orchard House, Inc., New Orleans, La.)

year. In addition to taking the tests, you may also have filled in a "personal profile" form listing your interests and personal characteristics. Each college selects thousands of candidates that most match its own student profile to recruit, and that's why you'll receive a lot of material from colleges you did not even consider.

As all this material arrives, pore through it and reduce your list to no more than a dozen colleges. In reading the material, remember that each college viewbook usually emphasizes the school's approach to education, as well as listing the kinds of courses and activities at the college. A viewbook invariably presents the most colorful, most pleasant picture possible of college life. It seldom lists negatives, but it does stress what college officials consider most important. You'll quickly learn from such viewbooks, as well as course catalogs, whether the emphasis is on preprofessional training, liberal arts, science or a combination of these.

One viewbook, for example, might stress that most of its students study biological sciences, economics and engineering, while the "core curriculum" at another university might consist of literature, history, social analysis and moral reasoning, science, and foreign cultures. And still another university might stress in its viewbook the wide range of business administration courses. So, study the descriptive material from each college carefully. It can provide you with valuable information and insights to help you make some of the key decisions mentioned earlier.

College Visits

To narrow your list of colleges still further, visit each school that interests you. The winter and spring vacations of your junior year are perfect times for such visits. Almost all colleges and universities offer guided tours to the public, usually led by friendly student guides who gladly answer questions honestly and openly (far more honestly, at times, than university officials do).

Telephone in advance to find out the days and hours of each college tour. Then plan an itinerary for visiting as many colleges as possible. Such tours offer you an opportunity to learn a great deal about each school without making any personal commitment. Remember, though, tours have no connection with the admissions process and are unrelated to visits for personal interviews you may want to have later on.

You may be upset at the idea of spending your spring vacation visiting colleges, but there are a number of important reasons for doing it. First of all, most colleges will still be in session. You'll be able to visit classes, talk with students, eat in the student cafeteria, and see life as it really is rather than as college officials and college brochures say it is. If you wait until summer, only the administration offices may be open. The faculty and students may be gone, and you'll see nothing but empty buildings and deserted lawns. At the colleges that are open, many of the students there will be adults taking adult education courses. You won't, in other words, get a feel for undergraduate student life as it really is during the part of the year when you'll be attending.

What's more, if you wait until summer in the northernmost areas of the country, you'll see every college at its picture-book best—green and flowery—at a time of year when you won't live there. By visiting in winter or early spring, you'll see the school at the time of year you'll have to spend there. The small, rural New England college that looks so pretty in viewbook pictures may seem desperately forlorn and isolated under a bleak, icy drizzle in February or March.

Many college vacations, of course, coincide with high school vacations. So be sure to check that the colleges you want to visit will be in session when you go. If not, ask your guidance counselor if your high school offers excused absences to visit colleges during the school term.

Among the key questions you should ask your guide on a college tour is whether there is an on-campus crime problem. Ask for a crime profile, which all colleges are obligated by law to issue. Ask about campus security and whether there is a drug problem on campus. How is the food? What are some of the things the student guide does *not* like at the college? How great are the academic pressures? Was this the tour guide's own first choice of college? From among the student guide's close friends, how many made this college their first choice? Remember to pick colleges you really want to attend, even for your second, third and fourth choices. If you've carefully and correctly picked the colleges you apply to, you should feel as pleased and excited if you're accepted at your safety school as you would be if you were accepted at your reach school.

I'm sure you and your parents will come up with many more questions of your own. A good thing to do is write questions down as you read through the college catalogs and then ask them when you tour each campus. Remember: College officials will want to know everything about you and your family before they admit you. So, before you go to the time and expense of applying, you owe it to yourself to be certain you know as much as you can about them and their schools. You should want to visit and learn about library, classroom, laboratory, art, music, dance, athletic and all other facilities, especially in areas of greatest interest to you. What opportunities does the college offer in the way of entertainment—theater, concerts, ballet, etc.? How difficult is transportation to and from college? How much crime is there on campus and in the surrounding community? What kinds? The questions are endless. Ask them all. Don't for a moment hesitate or be embarrassed to ask any question—and don't be embarrassed at or try to prevent your parents from asking questions on their minds. Sometimes one of their questions may give you a surprisingly different perspective on a particular school.

One question that's particularly important to ask your student guide, as well as admissions office representatives, is the percentage of courses taught by teaching assistants (TAs) instead of professors and instructors. TAs are graduate students who often have little or no experience as teachers and only a fraction of the knowledge of full-time faculty. Some TAs are only slightly older than you!

Years ago, TAs were hired only to correct exams or help guide science students with their laboratory experiments. As professors grew busier doing research and writing, they turned over some teaching duties to their assistants, often asking them to read lectures to classes. Now TAs have actually replaced professors in many classes—to save colleges big money over the costs of hiring professors.

If you want to get the best possible education, however, it's hardly worth spending $25,000 or more a year at a university that staffs its undergraduate classes with TAs instead of giving you the benefit of the wisdom and teaching skills of talented, experienced senior faculty. At several prestigious Ivy League colleges, TAs teach 25 percent or more of all undergraduate courses. Parents and students are complaining loudly—as well they should.

In contrast, smaller, highly selective "teaching colleges," such as Amherst, Bowdoin, Middlebury, Williams and many others, provide full-time faculty to *every* undergraduate in *every* course! Some of these great schools are more selective than others, but almost all teaching colleges will provide you with better teaching, and, in the long run, a better education than you'll ever get at many of the bigger universities that staff their undergraduate classes with TAs.

If you're a self-starter who can educate yourself, by all means go to a big university, where you'll be largely responsible for your own education. But if you want and need skilled faculty to involve themselves actively in your education, go to a teaching college, with small classes and skilled professors—many of them as famous as those at the great research universities—who love teaching and want to teach you!

You will have to spend four years of your life and more than $100,000 going to college. You owe it to yourself and your family to spend at least as much time and effort learning about and shopping for a college as you would, say, for a new car—which costs far less and will have far less long-term effect on the course of your future life. With the possible exception of your future home, university education will probably represent the biggest single investment you will ever make—which is why I believe so strongly in visiting each of the colleges that interest you twice, if you can: once during your initial selection process, for an overall guided tour and a meeting with admissions officials to eliminate a few schools from your list; a second time for an overnight stay in the dorms with freshmen and a chance to sample all aspects of life at that college, including classes.

Special Students

If you're physically disadvantaged or have special learning differences, be certain to explore college campuses somewhat more carefully. If you have physical disadvantages, for example, be certain that the campuses you consider are barrier free and that you have easy access to every area of the campus and every facility you might need. Be certain that recreational as well as academic and extracurricular facilities are all easily accessible. Although laws require all educational institutions to be accessible to physically disadvantaged students, faculty and staff, many institutions are careless, negligent or in outright violation of such laws—often because they don't want to or can't spend the huge funds required to accommodate what is often a tiny minority. If that's the case at any campus you visit, don't waste your valuable time trying to force them into compliance. Simply find the college that's right for you.

Similarly, if you're a student with learning differences such as dyslexia, find out, in advance, whether the college and its faculty can accommodate you in a way that will allow you to take full advantage of college learning experiences—both in and out of the classroom. If you're a gifted student, ask whether the college routinely allows gifted students to move ahead at a swifter-than-conventional pace. For example, Yale University allows gifted students to complete their undergraduate programs in less than three years and move ahead to graduate studies while remaining with their original friends and classmates on the undergraduate campus. At the end of four years, they attend graduation ceremonies with their original class, receiving, for example, an M.A. or other advanced degrees along with their bachelor's degrees.

So, as you visit campuses, be a smart and demanding consumer, making certain, at every step of the way, whether the college will be able to meet *your* needs. You know you're going to have to meet the admission requirements of each college. Make certain that they meet yours as well. Remember: You're a paying customer!

Making College Visits Fun

A way to make college visits—especially the tours—more fun is to make them family outings and spread them over your entire junior year. Your family could, for example, spend a weekend in historic Boston, touring several of the area's great universities and even taking in a collegiate sporting event. A trip to Philadelphia and Constitution Hall could include a stop at Princeton and the University of Pennsylvania, while a visit to Elizabethtown College, in Elizabethtown, Pa., could tie in with an exciting tour of the historic Civil War battlefield at nearby Gettysburg.

Whichever way you plan your college visits—and there are many ways—the important thing to keep in mind is that selecting which schools to apply to, and, ultimately, the one you finally attend, are decisions that will affect your entire life. If you were buying a home you'd certainly visit it and the neighboring community at least three times before buying it. I think it's just as important to do the same thing before "buying" a college education. Thousands of college students drop out every year because they made a poor choice of college. Make your choice the right one. Spend the extra time and money to make sure it's right.

Off-Campus Contacts

There are several other types of rather easy contacts you can make with the colleges. While they may only provide you with a superficial description, they can be worthwhile.

Each year, admissions office representatives from around the country visit most private and public schools that send a significant percentage of their students to college, to give a brief talk about their programs. Often, the discussion is followed by a video about the college as well as a helpful question-and-answer session. Although attendance at such meetings usually entitles high school seniors to cut classes, I believe juniors should also attend them because they are the ones who really should begin getting an introductory sense of what each college is like. So, if you can obtain permission from your guidance counselor to attend such meetings as a junior, I think they'll provide you with a lot of help in narrowing down the list of colleges to which you'll later want to apply. Make certain to give the admissions representatives your name and address so that they can send you additional materials—but tell them you're only a junior if that's the case. Then, sit back and listen carefully and take notes.

Be sure to ask questions (intelligent ones, of course). Ask especially about the percentage of undergraduate courses taught by teaching assistants instead of senior faculty. Don't dominate the question period or sound argumentative. Show interest, not hostility. The admissions office representative will certainly note your interest, and it might go down as a plus in your application folder.

Still another kind of contact you can make with admissions offices of some colleges is at the receptions to which you (and sometimes your parents) may be invited. They're usually held in private banquet rooms of local hotels. They, too, usually include videos about the colleges and question-and-answer sessions for students who want to learn more about the sponsoring college and may not be able to visit the campus. Don't, however, waste precious study time on such receptions unless you're truly interested in learning more about a particular college.

A third, preliminary, off-campus contact you can make with colleges is at so-called college fairs. Held in high schools and meeting halls across the country, such fairs bring together representatives from a wide variety of colleges and universities. Each college usually has its own exhibit and one or more representatives who willingly describe their schools and hand out reams of information.

There are two other important factors to consider in narrowing the list of colleges to which you'll eventually apply. One is cost and the other is your own high school grade point average (GPA).

Cost Consideration

I'll only deal briefly here with costs, and save most of the details on financing your college education for Chapter 5. The important thing to keep in mind right now, though, is that costs should in no way influence your college selection and application process. *Financial need is no reason not to go to college. Nor is it a reason not to apply to the most prestigious, most costly colleges.*

Every solvent college and university offers direct scholarship grants, financial aid and on-campus work opportunities to help underwrite the costs of attending. There is also a wide variety of low-interest student loans available, which do not have to be repaid until you're out of college and working. Students from the lowest income groups—even students without any family support—are now attending colleges costing $20,000 a year or more.

None of the prestigious, highly selective colleges that want you will keep you out because you don't have adequate funds. They will all see to it that you have an adequate "financial package" so that you can spend your college years free of worries about money. Many such colleges and universities strictly observe a "need-blind" admissions policy—that is, they don't even look at your financial circumstances in considering your admissions applications. "No student who is considering Yale should hesitate to apply because of financial circumstances," says Yale's admissions staff. "An application for financial aid will have no bearing on the Admission Committee's decisions."

Harvard makes the same invitation: "If Harvard and Radcliffe offer the undergraduate experience you want, we encourage you to apply regardless of family financial resources." Harvard's average scholarship award was more than $11,000 in the 1993–94 school year—more than 60 percent of the tuition. About 74 percent of the students at Harvard and 67 percent of the students at Stanford receive some sort of financial aid. These are two of America's costliest colleges, with tuition, room, board and other costs more than $25,000 a year. They also happen to be among the wealthiest schools, with more than enough resources to help finance the education of students they feel are qualified. A less costly, less selective college with fewer resources might be unable to offer you enough financial aid to cover all your college costs, and you'd have to fill that financial gap yourself.

For families in the lowest income category (less than $15,000 in total annual family income), the most competitive private colleges often cover more than 80 percent of total college costs. Some cover 100 percent! In addition to direct scholarship grants, they help arrange student loans (either direct loans from the college, or bank loans and federal loans, if the student is eligible) and on-campus and off-campus work opportunities. Students receiving aid are, of course, expected to contribute some of their own earnings to their education where possible—usually about $4,000 a year, through loans and on-campus and summer jobs. About 75 percent of Harvard students had jobs during a recent school year, earning an average of more than $1,000.

So, if you're going to need financial aid, ask your guidance office for appropriate forms and information. This is one area in which your high school guidance counselor should be able to offer you a lot of help by supplying you with literature and applications for a wide variety of scholarships, government and state grants, and student loans. One book that might be helpful is the *College Cost Book*, which is published annually by the College Entrance Examination Board. It outlines most major financial aid programs available to college-bound students. You can also get lots of information about financial aid from the colleges themselves when you write for viewbooks and other information. They'll send you complete details, and when they send you the admissions applications, they'll include the appropriate financial aid applications for you and your family to fill out. Asking for financial aid will probably not affect your admission chances at all. If any of the selective colleges accept you, that means they want you, and most of them will find a way to help you obtain the necessary funds.

I don't want to minimize the importance of costs, but the problem of paying for a college education is one that will almost certainly take care of itself once you gain admission to the college of your choice—especially if you are forthright and honest about your financial needs throughout the application process. Chapter 5 gives you more details about financing your college education. For now, though, put cost considerations aside. Honestly—they are nothing to worry about.

Grade Point Average Requirements

Your GPA is a problem only you can deal with—and indeed should have started dealing with during your freshman year in high school. In general, any of the college selection aids I've listed earlier and the profiles issued by the colleges themselves can serve as useful guides in determining whether your GPA measures up to the requirements of each college on your list. Don't use the guidelines in such selection aids as hard and fast rules, however. *Barron's*, for example, states that the most competitive colleges and universities require that applicants "in general" rank in the top 10 percent to 20 percent of their high school classes and have averages of A to B+. Keep in mind, though, that "in general" does not mean *all*. The most competitive colleges often enroll students who only finish in the top 25 percent of their classes and sometimes even lower. Much depends on the individual student and the type of high school he or she attended and the level of the courses taken.

In the next chapter, we'll discuss in detail how colleges select their students. My only reason for bringing up GPA now is to emphasize its importance in helping you select a list of a half-dozen or more colleges that interest you the most. If you rank in the bottom half of your high school class, there is almost no point in applying to a college that demands applicants who rank in the top 10 percent of their high school classes. If, on the other hand, you rank in the top 25 percent or even the top 30 percent, don't count yourself out of the most competitive group of colleges, especially if your ranking has been rising steadily and improving with age and maturity. Depending on your other qualifications and personal qualities, you may stand a good chance of getting in, and such colleges should be kept on your list.

Your final list of colleges should consist of no more than eight. To apply to more than eight is costly and unnecessary. Application fees are as much as $50, and you're only going to attend one college. (High school guidance counselors can obtain fee waivers for students who show financial need.) By using all the selection aids suggested in this chapter, you should be able to narrow your list to the six or eight colleges that are best for you.

By all means apply to one, two or even three reach schools, and two or three colleges whose typical students' characteristics and academic histories pretty well match your own. And finally, pick one or two safety schools—colleges you'd truly like to attend, but ones where your academic strengths will clearly rank you in the top third or quarter of the student body, thus practically assuring you of admission. But be certain that your safety schools differ from your reach schools only in their admissions requirements—not in the other qualities that made your reach schools your top choices. In other words, it's important that you pick your safety schools (and perhaps attend one) with the same enthusiasm as you would any other college you apply to.

SUMMARY

1. Early planning
2. Entrance requirements
3. College curriculum
   a. Preprofessional
   b. Liberal arts and sciences
   c. Combined preprofessional and arts and sciences

4. Choosing a college environment
   a. Large university or small college
   b. City, suburbs or country
   c. Distance from home
   d. Coed or single-sex
   e. Living conditions
      i) Single room or roommates
      ii) On- or off-campus
      iii) Dorms or apartments
   f. Extracurricular activities

5. Level of college difficulty
   a. Admissions
   b. Course work

6. Selection aids
   a. *Barron's Profiles of American Colleges*; Cass and Birnbaum's *Comparative Guide to American Colleges*; Peterson's *Guide to Four-Year Colleges*; and individual college profiles from the *College Admissions Data Handbook*, the College Board's *College Handbook*, computer programs in your guidance office, or the colleges themselves
   b. College viewbooks, catalogs, brochures and profiles
   c. Campus tours and visits
      i) Talks with students and student guides
      ii) Talks with school officials and faculty
   d. Cost considerations
      The College Board's College Cost Book
   e. GPA requirements

COLLEGE ADMISSION 3
REQUIREMENTS: PUTTING TOGETHER THE RIGHT "PACKAGE"

By now, you should have reduced your list of prospective colleges to no more than eight. You've picked those eight on the basis of decisions you've made about the college curriculum and college environment that appeal to you most. You've also chosen your list on the basis of realistic chances of getting in. Your high school GPA is the most important factor in gaining admission to the college of your choice, but there are many, many others. We'll discuss each of them in detail. But first and foremost, it's those grades that count.

"What a student does five days a week for 32 weeks a year over three and a half years simply cannot be discounted," explains Ronald D. Potier, director of admissions, Elizabethtown College, Elizabethtown, Pa. "The most important single item that a student can present to a competitive college is his high school record. The depth of the curriculum and how the student responds to that curriculum is the first thing a competitive college looks at."

So, if you're only a freshman or sophomore, or even a junior in the opening weeks of the first term, you can still change your work habits and your approach to school work to boost your grades. If you're at all interested in getting into any of the most selective colleges and universities listed in the top categories in *Barron's*, there is no way to overemphasize the importance of grades and course selection. They are the first thing college admissions officers examine in your application package. They probably won't even look at the rest of your application if your grades don't measure up to minimum standards. Grades will be an important question in any meeting you have with college admissions representatives. "What kind of grades are you getting?" is a standard question in almost every interview, whether it's with an admissions officer or an alumnus. (We'll discuss interviews in depth later.)

But college admissions officers are understanding people and they are aware that most 14- and 15-year-olds are not as mature as most 16- and 17-year-olds. So, they'll forgive a less-than-successful freshman year high school GPA, with the understanding that many 14- and 15-year-olds fail to take academic life seriously.

What they usually won't forgive is a poor junior year. Even if sophomore grades were less than sterling, they'll forgive that too, if, in junior year and in the first half of senior year, a student shows marked improvement and, in effect, begins working at his or her full potential. Ideally, they'd like to see a consistent 4.0 average over the first three and one-half years of high school, but they realize that's rare. So they're usually willing to judge a student with, say, a 2.7 freshman year, a 3.2 sophomore year and a 3.6 junior year as a 3.6 student. They view a record of *steady improvement* as that of a normal, healthy young person displaying ever-increasing maturity with each passing year. The first half of senior year, of course, will have to be the clincher. If the student's grades drop, the chances of getting into a highly competitive college will all but disappear. If, on the other hand, the student maintains a 3.6 average or improves it during the first half of senior year, the chances of getting into a selective college will improve. Obviously, I'm only using these figures as an example. There are many other combinations of grades that would gain our hypothetical student admission to a first-choice college. The important thing, however, is for you to show steady improvement in grades, consistent with increasing age and maturity.

In conjunction with that, I can't emphasize enough the importance of *NOT LETTING DOWN* during your senior year. The temptations to do so will be enormous. The football games—your last ever at your old school; the extracurricular activities; driving privileges; the increased number of parties; and the sheer excitement of being a senior can make it all too easy to ignore your academic work. But try to remember this: *The work you do during the first half of your senior year can be critical and could decide whether or not you get into the college of your choice.*

THE APPLICATION "PACKAGE"

Although GPA is the most important factor in college admissions, it is but one of almost two dozen elements that college admissions committees examine in weighing what they call your application package. They call it that because your folder will indeed be as thick as a package by the time your application is complete, with all your high school data and recommendations, and with all the interview and discussion notes that they'll add to it.

A "perfect package" would be an application from a student with a four-year GPA of 4.0, combined SAT scores of 1,600, 800 in each of three SAT II Tests, and Advanced Placement (AP) scores of 5 in each of five subjects—and the student is also a team captain in three sports, class president, holds down a job to support himself, and volunteers to deliver meals to shut-ins. Obviously, few packages are perfect, and colleges weigh all elements in relation to the total package —the total human being—before putting it in the "accept" or "reject" or "wait-list" category.

In addition to GPA, other elements in each package include course quality, average class rank, SAT I and II scores or ACT scores, AP test scores, extracurricular activities in school, out-of-school activities (jobs, community contributions, sports, summer camp, travel), unusual activities or characteristics that make you unique, factors beyond your control that give your application preferred status, your application itself, your essays, the recommendations of your teachers and your guidance counselor, and possibly your personal interview.

Every college has its own rating system that places a specific value on each of these factors and then adds them up to produce a total value for each applicant package. It should be evident that, with so many factors, few applicants can achieve a perfect score. For any applicant, a high rating in one area can often balance a low rating in another. Almost any college will pay less attention to low SAT I scores of a student with a high GPA *and* high SAT II scores *and* high AP test scores.

By now, you must be getting an idea of how complex the process of reviewing college applications really is, and how difficult the decisions admissions officers must make are. Most are dedicated, caring people who are truly trying to match the right applicants to the right colleges. They are not, in other words, "gatekeepers" trying to keep students out. But those at the most selective schools have no choice but to reject at least half their applicants, because they simply don't have the space—even for all the applicants who could do the work.

Lack of space, though, is not the only reason many qualified applicants are rejected. Admissions officers assume that most applicants *can* do the work. What they want to know is whether applicants *will* do the work *and* also make a contribution to the college.

Yale University's admissions office puts it this way:

> Most applicants to Yale are well qualified in academic terms, but only a few are so accomplished academically that they are admitted on those grounds alone. The most important questions the Admissions Committee must resolve are "Who is likely to make the most of Yale's resources?" and "Who will contribute significantly to the Yale community?" . . . In sum, qualifications include not only the reasonably well-defined areas of academic achievement and special skills in non-academic areas, but also the less tangible qualities of capacity for involvement, commitment, and personal growth. None of these can be measured precisely. . . .

In other words, applicants who apply to such prestigious, selective colleges must be able to prove that they deserve admission by reason of the quality of their academic work *and* the contributions they've made to their communities while at high school. There's no question that college admissions officers do make mistakes, but they try their best to base all their decisions on what they feel will serve the best interests of both student and college. Incidentally, the long list of package elements should also give you an indication of why most high school guidance counselors and college advisers simply do not have enough time to help each of their students put together a package that will assure admission to reach schools.

DEVELOPING YOUR APPLICATION PACKAGE

You, however, have the time to develop the kind of application package you'll need, and it's up to you to do it. Let's start at the top and examine all the elements of the package and see how they're weighed by college admissions people. To do this, it's essential that you now go to your public library or your guidance counselor's office and make copies of the profiles of the colleges that most interest you in the *College Admissions Data Handbook (CADH)*. Much of the information in those profiles can be found in *Barron's*, Cass and Birnbaum, *Peterson's*, or the *College Handbook*, of course, but it's often more difficult and time consuming to find it and dig it out. The *CADH* profiles are neatly organized and somewhat easier to use once you've narrowed your list of colleges. All the *CADH* data comes directly from admissions officers. Each profile gives you an indication of how much weight that particular college will put on each element of your package. You'll see, too, that the factors each college lists as most important under "Basis for Candidate Selection" are divided into two categories: The foremost is "Academic" and the secondary group of factors is simply called "Other." So, you can use the *CADH* profiles as guides in helping you understand what constitutes a good college admissions package. If *CADH* profiles are not easily available to you, ask your guidance office if they have any of the computer programs issued by Guidance Information Services, the College Board or Peterson. These, too, offer fairly good individual profiles of most colleges, although *CADH* is generally considered best.

As we look at the elements that make up a good applicant package, let's see, too, if there's anything you can do to improve each element of your package.

Grades

As I said earlier, your GPA is all-important. Look at the *CADH* profile for the University of Michigan (pp. 00–00), which is ranked in *Barron's* second category of "Highly Competitive" colleges and universities. Under the section entitled "Basis for Candidate Selection," secondary school record, SAT or ACT scores, class rank, and school's recommendation are listed in that order as the four key academic factors they take into consideration in deciding whether to accept an applicant. A little bit farther along in the profile, you'll see that 92 percent of a recent freshman class ranked in the top fifth of their high school classes, and only six percent ranked in the second fifth. So, if you rank in the third or fourth fifth of your high school class, your chances of getting into Michigan are slim.

It's much the same story at other competitive schools. About 80 percent of the candidates accepted in a recent freshman class at Scripps College, Claremont, Calif., ranked in the top fifth of their high school classes. Scripps is listed in *Barron's* second highest category of "Highly Competitive" colleges. At Harvard and Radcliffe colleges, 98 percent of a recent freshman class ranked in the top fifth of their high school classes, while 95 percent of Stanford freshmen, 97 percent of Amherst freshmen and 95 percent of Northwestern freshmen ranked in the top fifth of their high school classes. These and other top-ranked colleges all list secondary school record first among the factors used as a basis for candidate selection. So, if you're aiming to get into schools of that caliber, start working in your freshman or sophomore year for the best possible grades you can get. As I said earlier, it's not too late to start now, even if you're still a junior. If you're already a senior and you've had poor grades until now but know you can do better, think about a two-year project to score a startling comeback this year and then repeat senior year next year with higher-level courses.

Course Quality

I'm sure you know that a B in regular math is not worth a B in honors math for the same age group. So course quality is a factor to take into consideration when you use your GPA to determine whether to apply to a particular college or university. College admissions officers will know the academic level of every course you take. If you want to prepare for a competitive college, make certain you take the highest-level courses your high school offers, if you're able to do so comfortably and continue to achieve relatively high grades. A D in an honors course is not worth an A in the comparable standard course for the same year. So don't overreach. Try to take the most challenging courses you can handle, and don't waste time with nonacademic electives. Stick to traditional courses in English, history, math, modern languages and sciences. In addition to honors courses, take AP courses wherever possible if you're qualified and if they're available in your high school. I'll discuss more about AP courses later.

Class Rank

In addition to your GPA, your class ranking can be an important factor, because it can help to put your school's grading system in proper perspective. For example, a 3.9 GPA and a class ranking of 12th would indicate that your teachers gave out high grades pretty liberally. Similarly, a 3.5 GPA and a ranking of first or second would mean that your school grading system is pretty tough (although it could also mean that your class isn't very bright!). Most top colleges have computer records that correlate college performance with high school GPAs and class rankings for previous students from your school.

The SAT

How important are Scholastic Assessment Test (SAT) scores? That's a question every guidance counselor, college adviser and college admissions officer hears a thousand times a year. Let me try to answer the question for you. In some cases they're all-important; in a few cases they have limited importance. Most selective colleges list SAT scores among the most important factors they consider in selecting candidates for admission. That's because SATs and other entrance examinations set a common standard for students throughout the country regardless of race, creed, color or religion; regardless of the schools they attend; and regardless of whether, as in some cases, teachers give favored students higher grades than they deserve and thus improve their chances of getting into college. (Few teachers consciously give students higher grades than they deserve, of course. What often happens, though, is that they pay more attention and give more encouragement to students they feel, rightly or wrongly, have a better chance of success at college—just as college advisers often pay more attention to athletic and academic stars.)

The SATs measure everybody by the same yardstick: the same questions given under the same testing conditions. For a student with a less-than-startling GPA of 2.6, combined SAT I and SAT II scores of 1,500 will indicate he has far more potential than he has shown in high school. In combination with a great application essay, perhaps a successful personal interview, some strong letters of recommendation, and a few other favorable elements, his high SAT scores may be enough to convince some colleges to take a chance on him. On the other hand, other colleges might conclude that, with the potential evident in his SAT scores, the student has obviously handled his high school work immaturely and failed to do his best. Such colleges might not take a chance on him.

Some colleges put greater stock in SAT scores than others, because those scores have always served them as strong indicators of how well any given student will ultimately perform at the college level. Turning to the University of Michigan *CADH* profile in Chapter 2, you can see that class rank and SAT scores are featured among the four most important elements under "Basis for Candidate Selection."

Harvard University, on the other hand, puts less emphasis on SAT and ACT scores, saying, "There are no score cutoffs; we do not admit 'by the numbers.'" Its primary emphasis is on "academic talent," although it adds, "Good grades are only part of the picture . . . we also look for evidence of energy, innovation, creativity. . . ."

Yale University takes a slightly different tack. Although it considers SAT scores important, it emphasizes that even the highest SAT scores may be worthless if you get poor grades in high school. "While there is no hard and fast rule," says Yale's booklet on admissions, "it is safe to say that performance is relatively more important [than] testing. A very strong performance in a demanding college preparatory program may compensate for modest standardized test scores, but it is unlikely that high test scores will persuade the Admissions Committee to disregard an undistinguished secondary-school record."

Similarly, Colgate University, a prestigious college in Hamilton, New York, lists SAT scores and other standardized tests as less important than "the number and level of difficulty of courses taken during the high school years . . . [the applicant's] academic performance . . . the observations of teachers and secondary school counselors, and . . . applicants' presentations of themselves." That last element refers to the quality of your application and essay and to the skills you demonstrate in your interviews with admissions officers and alumni. I'll discuss both application and interviews in Chapter 4.

All of which brings us back to that original puzzling question: How important are the SAT scores? Quite simply, it depends on the individual student and his total application package. The most prestigious colleges in America will give less importance to low SAT I scores of a student with a high GPA who consistently scores 700 or more in all his SAT II tests. Or, in the case of the junior who is able to take AP courses in his junior year, scores of 4 and 5 in AP tests will almost certainly offset low SAT I scores.

Most colleges recognize the dangers of overreliance on SAT I scores, because they tend to measure a student's ability to respond instantly to prepared questions, while failing to gain a true measure of his other knowledge. Even SAT administrators recognize this. In fact, students with dyslexia and other learning differences who cannot handle instant-response tests, can take specially administered untimed SATs. If you have dyslexia or some other learning difference, have your physician certify that to your school and insist that they arrange for you to take an untimed SAT. (Some schools grumble a bit, because it puts them to extra trouble to set up special testing arrangements for only one student. But insist on it, and don't let anyone tell you such a test does not exist. It does.)

The SATs are administered on Saturdays, but if your religion forbids your taking them on the regularly scheduled date, you can ask to take the test on the following Sunday.

If your SAT (or PSAT) scores are low, by all means get some tutoring and then take them a second time. The Educational Testing Service, which puts together and grades the tests, claims that tutoring usually won't help you improve your SAT scores significantly. But there are many students whose SAT scores have improved significantly after such tutoring. So, I feel it's worth the effort and expense. You've got everything to gain and nothing to lose. Regardless of how many times you take the SATs, most colleges only take your two highest scores into consideration in evaluating your application.

If you can't afford tutoring, you can buy books or software with old SATs to get some practice in taking this kind of test. Most of these books also have important prefaces on how to take such tests. Time limitations make almost everyone nervous, and practice can help.

SAT II Tests

Some colleges put more weight than others on SAT II scores, and their viewbooks (and your college selection aids) usually make their importance quite clear. Some colleges require three SAT II tests as the equivalent of entrance examinations. Colgate University, for example, requires three SAT II tests, but allows applicants to take five and then skip taking the SAT I tests.

The SAT II tests measure knowledge in particular subjects and are tests for which you can prepare yourself quite thoroughly through hard work and study. Tutoring in SAT II tests can often prove extremely valuable, because it can increase the body of knowledge needed for high scores; and high SAT II scores can often compensate for low SAT I scores. By all means buy the appropriate books or software available for preparing for SAT II tests. *Barron's*, for example, publishes a dozen such books for various subjects.

You can take SAT II tests in more subjects than most colleges require and then release only those with the highest scores. In other words you could, for example, take SAT II tests in six subjects and send only those three with the highest scores to colleges requiring three.

Remember, though, that SAT II tests demand rapid responses, and some students with great knowledge simply don't have the knack—or maybe the cool nerves—to snap out short answers correctly under the pressure of tight time restrictions. For such students, AP exams can be a key to a successful college application—especially students who are indeed scholars in one or more fields. In many cases, high AP scores can offset low SAT I and SAT II scores. (See Appendix D for a more complete explanation of SAT I and SAT II tests and other college entrance examinations.)

AP Tests

Freshmen, sophomores, juniors and seniors who have completed specially designed AP courses in high school can take AP tests. AP courses are advanced, college-level courses given to high school students who have completed their entire high school curriculum in those courses. AP courses measure a student's ability to function at the college level—as do the AP tests. So, many colleges give AP scores greater weight than they do SAT or Achievement Test scores.

Unfortunately, few high school students are eligible to take AP courses, and some schools don't even offer them. If your school does offer them, and you're an exceptional enough student to take them, try to do so in your junior year. It's rare, of course, that a junior has accumulated enough knowledge to take a college-level AP course, especially in areas such as history, English, or math, which require three or more years of high school preparation. But if, in your sophomore year, you've done exceptionally well in the most advanced high school-level course offered in a subject, by all means take the AP course in your junior year. That way, you'll be able to put the AP test scores in your application and have them influence the college admissions decision.

A nice thing about AP tests, by the way, is that you're not required to list them on your applications, and the Educational Testing Service does not automatically send them to colleges. There's no need to take an AP course in every subject. AP tests are scored on a scale of 1 to 5, and a 4 or 5 in even one test—history, for example—will indicate that you placed among the nation's top high school scholars in that subject. Such a score shows that you're obviously a superior student and more than able to handle college-level work. Unlike instant-response tests, AP tests ask you for in-depth, essay-type answers to complex questions. That's why a high AP test score can often offset low SAT I or SAT II scores. A high AP test score also often allows admissions officers to give your high school's quality rating a bit less weight in judging your application, because AP tests measure you against national college-level scholarship, not by the quality of your particular high school.

If you take AP courses in your senior year, you won't be able to take the AP tests until spring, after the colleges have already decided on your applications and too late to affect those decisions. The fact that you took AP courses, however, will appear on your school transcript and show you to be an above-average scholar—even without any AP test scores.

Although AP tests in the spring of your senior year won't affect your college admissions, they can affect college course placement levels. Many colleges use AP test scores for placement purposes and permit students with high scores to skip the freshman requirement in that subject and begin at the sophomore level. Such an exemption may count as a full college course credit toward graduation. Before studying for and taking an AP test at the end of your senior year of high school, however, *be certain the college you plan to attend does indeed give credits for APs.*

Extracurricular Activities

Extracurricular activities give admissions officers an indication of each student's interests, personality and ability to work with others. It also shows them how well and wisely you use your extra time, which is a reflection of maturity. Do you use your extra time to sleep or watch TV or go to the mall—or do you use it to improve yourself by taking up interesting hobbies or by making significant contributions to your family and your community? Exceptional achievements in extracurricular activities rarely offset bad grades, but they can add weight to a package that includes average or slightly above-average grades and high SAT I and II test scores. An applicant with a 3.4 GPA who has a varsity letter in a major sport, is a class officer or the editor of his school newspaper will almost certainly get the nod over a student with a 3.6 GPA and no extracurricular activities—assuming all other elements of the two packages are equal.

Most colleges and universities list participation in extracurricular activities as one of the more important factors in considering candidates for admission, but the weight each college places on such activities differs.

There are several basic categories of extracurricular activities: athletic, nonathletic, in-school and out-of-school. Each category carries a different weight at different colleges, and by reading between the lines, you can generally infer from college viewbooks the importance each places on different types of extracurricular activity. In any case, here is an area in which you can easily improve your college application package. You don't have to make a varsity team or get the lead role in the drama society production. Participation, even if it's only in intramural sports or as an extra in the school play, is what counts most on your college application in this category.

Most students are not superstars in any area, and admissions officers must examine and weigh each element of each package to determine the applicants they believe will best function at each particular college. Most admissions officers favor applicants with a wide variety of interests, skills and talents, and a strong sense of obligation to his or her community. But, *be careful* not to misinterpret this as meaning that these colleges necessarily favor the so-called well-rounded student, who, according to one dean of admissions, is like a "goose egg: smooth, wholesome, and scarcely discernible."

What all colleges seek is a well-rounded *student body*, not necessarily well-rounded students. They want a student body made up of unique individuals, each with unique talents and qualities that make that student stand out among most of his or her peers—qualities that will enrich the rest of the college class and the college community. So don't pay attention to the myth of the well-rounded student. It is only a myth spread by people who think they know something about the college admissions process but actually know little or nothing. The most competitive colleges select far more students on *academic achievement alone* than they do on the basis of participation in a wide variety of nonacademic activities.

Academic, artistic or athletic achievements are seen as measures of individual strengths, and many extracurricular activities are seen as nothing more than extensions of those interests. Some extracurricular activities, however, can add significant weight to an application package. The editorship of a school publication, for example—especially the newspaper—is often viewed as a major contribution to one's school community and an indication of a student's commitment to that community. Such an activity involves a lot of time and effort, with precious little personal reward. Class officerships often weigh a bit less, because usually they only reflect a student's popularity among his peers. There's nothing wrong with being popular, but popularity does not necessarily reflect maturity or effectiveness as a community leader. Class officerships must be paired with measurable accomplishments to have much value in the application package—accomplishments such as reform of the student dress code, for example, or establishment of antidrug or antialcohol programs. The admissions officers are less interested in whether you were a class officer than whether you were an *effective* class officer.

Participation in school performing arts groups is also viewed favorably, but, again, as evidence of one's individual talent rather than as a deep and lasting contribution to one's community.

In short, extracurricular activities do add weight to an applicant's package, because they display individual strengths that may not be evident in the classroom or on the playing fields. But the extracurricular activities that add the most weight are those that display a student's concern for and contributions to the community—without regard for personal rewards. In other words, colleges look at the quality of a student's extracurricular activities rather than the quantity.

Out-of-School Activities

Your activities outside school can also add weight to your application package. Selective colleges want to know how you spend your spare time—whether you spend it constructively, improving your own skills and talents and helping your community, or whether you simply vegetate in front of the TV screen or at the mall.

Like in-school extracurricular activities, those out-of-school activities that add the most weight are those that display your concern for your community. Harvard has always been quite blunt about it: "We place great value in a candidate's capacity to move beyond the limits of personal achievement to involvement in the life of the community at large. We seek candidates who demonstrate a willingness to take an interest in the lives and welfare of others or to place themselves in situations which call for personal initiative and leadership."

Almost all of the most selective and prestigious schools in the United States agree. Volunteer work over an extended period, participation in political campaigns and similar activities can add considerable weight to a college application package as measures of character and imagination. For example, a few years ago Williams College, in Massachusetts, accepted an early-decision candidate from New York City, who, completely on her own, had spent a summer organizing a summer theater group for underprivileged children in Manhattan. The project not only kept the children busy building sets, learning parts, acting and working behind the scenes, it helped them improve their reading and writing, and had positive effects on their school work as well. Her voluntary efforts, combined with a successful extracurricular acting career at her own school, added enough weight to a B academic average to earn her an early-decision acceptance. Williams is in *Barron's* highest-ranked group of "Most Competitive" colleges.

Another important outside activity is having a steady job each summer and even during the school year. This is so important that many colleges provide a separate section in the application for you to list your jobs and employers during your high school years. Such colleges know how much initiative it takes for teenagers to find temporary summer work, and they regard the ability to find a steady job and to contribute to one's support as an indication of maturity. And maturity is a key factor most colleges consider in deciding whether to accept a candidate. Indeed, many colleges list maturity second only to character and motivation among the elements they consider most important in candidate selection.

Sports participation outside school—skiing, sailing, etc.—is of interest in that it adds evidence of the applicant's wide-ranging interests, and these should be included in the applications. Camping, travel and other out-of- school experiences also contribute to each individual's background. While admissions officers take them all into consideration to some extent in weighing an applicant's package, don't expect such activities to compensate for bad grades or poor SAT scores.

Character

Most colleges and universities list character as the nonacademic quality they consider most important. One college dean of admissions defines *character* as "honesty, demonstration of social involvement, and a diligent approach to both academic and extracurricular life at school." Harvard College once defined it this way:

> Students applying to college do not always realize the significance of strong personal qualities and character in college admissions. Colleges are interested in more than students' achievements or skills. They seek to attract candidates who will contribute to the emotional and ethical climate of their undergraduate communities.
>
> We believe that educated men and women should aspire to develop integrity as well as intelligence during their high school years. In addition to artistic, athletic, extracurricular, and academic talent, we recognize in the admissions process the development of strong personal qualities. Our pluralistic and democratic society requires many qualities from its leaders as it seeks to meet the challenges of the years ahead; character is certainly one of them.

Now, that doesn't mean you won't get into a competitive school because you made a mistake when you were 10 or 12 or even 14. We all make mistakes. But if you're still having serious problems, with drugs or alcohol, for example, or have serious social or family problems, I strongly urge you to deal with and solve them first—before even considering attending college. Even if you get in, you simply won't be able to cope with the academic and social pressures while trying to handle serious personal problems. You'll either drop out or be expelled, and end up wasting thousands of dollars in nonrefundable fees— without solving your problems.

No matter what you may think, moving away from home, away from your parents to a "new life," won't solve any problems. That new life will simply add new problems to your old ones and make your life doubly difficult unless you solve those old problems first.

Recommendations

Recommendations—one or more from your teachers and a School Report (usually completed by your guidance counselor, college adviser or principal)—are also important elements of your application package. Many colleges list them as second in importance only to your grades—and ahead of both SAT I and SAT II scores. The School Report tends to have greater weight than teacher recommendations, however, because it is an evaluation of your overall high school performance. Teacher recommendations are usually based on only a year's contact with you, and may only reflect a teacher's fondness for a student instead of the student's ability to function at the college level.

College admissions people know that, and they know you'll pick teachers who like you most to write recommendations. The colleges expect those recommendations to be superb. Anything less than that could hurt you badly. If your teachers write bland recommendations or even slightly negative ones, the colleges will take them into serious consideration in evaluating your application. So, it's important to meet with your teachers *before* they write their recommendations—to get an idea of whether they feel they will give you good ones.

In selecting teachers, though, take into consideration the questions on the recommendation forms. Some applications ask the teacher to indicate which courses he or she taught you—and when. Colleges won't give much weight to a recommendation from a teacher who last taught you in ninth grade, when you were 13 or 14. So pick a teacher who has had a lot of contact with you during your junior year. For recommendation forms that ask the teacher about your academic work first and your general personality last, it's important to pick a teacher in whose course you've done exceptionally well. For forms that ask about your personality first and academic work second, be certain to select a teacher who knows you outside as well as inside the classroom.

By careful study of the questions colleges ask on the teacher recommendations and School Reports, you'll get a lot more insight into exactly what kind of student each college is seeking. Take a look in Chapter 4 at the Teacher's Evaluation form of the Common Application, which is used by several hundred colleges and universities, including the nation's most prestigious colleges such as Harvard. It asks the teacher to rate you on "creative, original thought, motivation, independence, initiative, intellectual ability, academic achievement, written expression of ideas, effective class discussion, disciplined work habits, and potential for growth." Obviously, the colleges and universities that now use the Common Application consider those the most important characteristics in candidates they plan to consider for admission.

So, use the forms to rate yourself, then make improvements where necessary.

In addition to meeting with teachers who will write your college recommendations, it's important to meet with the school official who will write your School Report—again, as early in your junior year as possible. Actually, you should have been meeting with your guidance counselor regularly since you entered high school. Remember, when the time comes to write the all-important School Report for your college applications your guidance counselor will only have a folder full of dry facts about your high school career, unless you've made the effort to get to know your counselor and to let your counselor know all about you—about your out-of-school activities, about those talents and qualities that make you a unique individual. I told you in Chapter 1 that you are unique—that we all are—and that it's those qualities that make you unique and different that may, in the end, determine whether you're the type of student the most prestigious colleges and universities are seeking.

Remember also that the three dozen most competitive colleges in America could fill every one of their classes exclusively with high school valedictorians (or class presidents)—and there would still be thousands of valedictorians (or class presidents) left over. The fact is that those colleges do not select students exclusively on grades, class rank and SAT scores, or extracurricular activities. Although these are all extremely important, the most prestigious colleges and universities are also looking for individuality—qualities that make you unique—and it's important that your guidance counselor or college adviser be aware of those qualities and write about them in the School Report that will go into your college application package.

There's another reason for meeting with your guidance counselor early in your junior year: to get an indication of what school officials think of you. If your guidance counselor, college adviser, or principal says he or she can't or won't give you a good recommendation, try to find out why and whether, with a supreme effort between now and the deadline for filing applications, you could display qualities—academic, social, behavioral—that could earn you a better recommendation.

In other words, if you've done less than your best until now, ask for an opportunity to turn over a new leaf and thus earn a better recommendation. Don't be afraid to negotiate! Your school officials do not want to block your entry into college. Indeed, they'll probably do everything they can to help you—as long as you show a willingness to help yourself by displaying superlative academic and social qualities and a sincere motivation to succeed. However, don't expect them to lie or even stretch the truth on your behalf. Remember, their own personal honor and the reputation of their school are at stake on every form they return to the colleges.

Be sure to take a close look at the School Report forms from each college, as well as the Teacher Recommendation forms. They also provide important clues to what the colleges are seeking in their candidates. Some colleges will ask the school for your class rank, first and foremost, but also ask for the size of your class. A rank of fifth would be far less impressive in a class of 20 than in a class of 100, depending on the academic ranking of your high school. They may also ask for such information as how long you've maintained your rank and whether your rank has been weighted (curved) or raised artificially, whether you've taken a tough academic program or not, and, significantly, how many students of your class plan to attend college. That's usually an indication of the academic level of a class.

Importance of Academics

One thing should now be clear to you. *Your academic perform-ance is the most important factor in gaining admission to the school of your choice.* The School Report of the Common Application is a good example of how important academic performance is for such colleges as Harvard, Cornell and hundreds of other fine schools. The first questions it asks your school counselor are your class rank, your grade point average, the academic strength of your class and the level of difficulty of your courses. It then asks the counselor to write what he or she considers important about you, starting with a description of *academic* and personal characteristics.

"We are particularly interested in the candidate's *intellectual* promise, motivation, integrity, independence, originality, in-itiative, leadership potential, capacity for growth, special tal-ents and enthusiasm." The italics are mine, to emphasize the importance of your work in the classroom.

Once again, *academics* are uppermost in the college applica-tion process at Harvard, Cornell and all the rest of the outstand-ing colleges that use the Common Application. That does not mean you won't get into such colleges without straight A's in honors-level courses. You certainly can, but you're going to have to compensate for lower grades with some superlative achievements in other areas.

In any case, be sure to use the questions on the School Report and the Teacher Recommendation forms as aids in weighing your own package and determining your chances of admission at each college. The questions on these forms can be a good indication of what each college is looking for most in its candi-dates.

To give you a little more insight into how to put together and evaluate your own package, stop for a moment, and put yourself in the office of the dean of admissions of a highly selective college, one that has applications from 12,000 qualified students and can only accept, say, 1,000. You have filled 999 seats and must weigh the packages of two candidates competing for the last opening. At a conference headed by the deans and directors of admission at Dartmouth College, Franklin & Marshall College, Harvard University, Lafayette College, Tufts University and the University of Pennsylvania, a group of high school guidance counselors was also asked to choose between these two hypothetical candidates. Which candidate would you choose, student A or student B?

The below example is aimed at showing you how difficult it is to select students for college admissions. There is no right or wrong answer, although you might like to know that Candidate B got the nod over Candidate A. Can you figure out why?

STUDENT A	STUDENT B
School: East-West H.S.	School: North-South H.S.
Rank: 53/550 (i.e., top 10%)	Rank: 62/630 (top 10%)
SAT I: V. 570; M. 640	SAT I: V. 590; M. 540
SAT II: 610 Eng. comp.	SAT II: 650 Eng. comp.
660 Math Level I	550 Math Level I
530 Chemistry	550 Math Level II
590 French	590 U.S. history

H.S. grades:

STUDENT A					STUDENT B				
English	A	A	B	A	English	A	B	A	A
Social studies	A	A	A	A	Social studies	B	A	A	A
Foreign language	B	B	A	B	Foreign language	B	B	A	A
Science	B	A	C	B	Science	A	–	A	A
Mathematics	A	B	A	A	Mathematics	B	B	B	–

School activities:

STUDENT A:
J.V. soccer (9, 10)
Monitor's squad (10, 11)
Class representative (10)
School newspaper (11)

STUDENT B:
J.V. field hockey (9, 10)
Varsity field hockey (11, 12)
School orchestra (9, 10, 11, 12)
First-chair flute (11, 12)
All-state orchestra (11, 12)
Youth symphony (4 yrs.)
Soloist (2 yrs.)

STUDENT A	STUDENT B
Community activities:	
Church youth group (6 yrs.)	
Baby-sitting (occasional)	
Travel (summers in U.S.)	
Work:	*Work:*
Part-time, father's law office	Farm field worker
during school year	(3 summers)
Ass't. counselor day camp	Manager on farm last
(one summer)	summer
	Volunteer, teen drug hot line
	(4 hrs./wk. current school year)

(Published courtesy of Anthony F. Capraro, Ph.D., president of Teach, The
Educational Search & Consulting Firm, and publisher of *The College Digest*,
both of Mamaroneck, New York.)

The Application Itself

Still another factor the admissions people weigh heavily in
considering your package is the application itself: Is it neatly
written or typed? What does the essay display that makes you
unique and therefore worthy of admission? We'll discuss these
questions in greater depth in the next chapter. For now, keep
in mind that the application and the essays you write in it are
key elements in your package and can be decisive in the admissions committee's deliberations on whether to admit you or
not—because they are two of the three elements in the admissions process that you can control yourself. (The other is the
personal interview, which we'll discuss later.) You have complete control over the neatness of your application, and you
have complete control over the essay you write. So these reflect
you and your personality, no one else's.

Other Recommendations

Years ago, most top-ranked colleges also asked for one or two
recommendations from people outside your school who knew
you well and could vouch for you. Many even asked that such
recommendations come from the alumni of the particular college. Naturally, applicants from the wealthiest, most powerful
families—with friends in the highest ranks of government,

business or the professions—had a great advantage over applicants from more average families. Almost all colleges and universities have now done away with this practice and indeed discourage it. Many admissions officers so resent outside pressures that they'll sometimes reject an otherwise acceptable applicant who tries to use outside connections to pressure his way into a college instead of getting in on his own merit. So don't include any outside recommendations with your application if your only aim is to pressure the admissions office into accepting you.

If, however, an outside recommendation can add weight to your application that might not otherwise show up, by all means include it. For example, if you performed some heroic act or valuable service for your community, you might not want to describe it yourself for fear of appearing conceited. You might then simply include "Mayor's Citation" in your list of community activities and major accomplishments, and include a copy—don't send the original—of the actual citation and, perhaps, copies of a newspaper clipping and personal letter from the mayor. You might also ask the mayor or his representative to write an independent letter of recommendation directly to the colleges. You might also want to write about it in your essay if you can do so without seeming conceited or pompous.

Personal Interview

A personal interview with an admissions officer at the college of your choice can be another important element in your package, because, like the application and essay, here is an element of the application process almost completely under your control. Again, we'll discuss this element in greater depth in the chapter on the application process, but for now, remember that the interview will not only give admissions people a chance to meet you personally, it will also serve as an indication of your motivation to attend that college. Most selective colleges list motivation or "desire to attend" among the most important nonacademic characteristics they seek in candidates. Unless you apply for "early decision" (see page 118), personal interviews are no longer required by most colleges, but there's no question that spending the time and money to travel to an out-of-the-way campus in Oregon, for example, or Vermont for a tour, an interview and an overnight visit will certainly be noted in your package as evidence of desire to attend.

In addition to an interview with an admissions officer or alumnus, an interview with a faculty member to apprise him or her of a special skill can also be valuable. If you're gifted in a particular subject, a special area or a particular sport, an interview with and recommendation from a faculty member or coach could prove decisive for your application.

Other Important Factors

Before proceeding to the application process, there are some other important factors you should be aware of. All are beyond your control, but, fairly or unfairly, they can influence your chances of admission.

HIGH SCHOOL QUALITY

There's one aspect of GPA, which, unfortunately, is beyond your control. Gertrude Stein said that "a rose is a rose is a rose," but a grade is not necessarily a grade in American schools, because grading standards vary dramatically from school to school. Indeed, a C at a selective high school or private prep school may be considered comparable to an A+ at an average public high school. That's sad but true—even if it's not the fault of students.

Whatever the reasons, the different *values* of grades at different schools are something that college admissions officers (and you) must consider in your application. One way they're able to rate the value of your grades is through use of a profile issued by your school (Figure 2). You should do the same thing. Ask your guidance counselor for a copy of your school's profile, the one they send to colleges. For public schools, at least, it is a public document and should be available either to you or your parents. Private school students can look up their school profiles in a book called *Peterson's Guide to Independent Secondary Schools*, which you can find in any major public library or book store.

Even if your school does not calculate class rankings, you can use your school profile to figure out where you stand and how college admissions people will interpret your grades. That interpretation will depend in large part on the school's grading system and the percentage of students who normally go to four-year colleges after graduation. A GPA of 80 at a school whose median GPA is 79.52 is hardly as impressive as an 80 in an equally large school with a median GPA of 70. Looking at it from another perspective, a 90 at a school where 20 percent of all students score 87.54 or higher is not as strong as a 90 in a school where only 10 percent, or even five percent, score only 87.54 or higher. So use the information from your high school's profile to put your own performance in proper perspective.

LEGACY

Another factor beyond your control is legacy. Legacy means you are the son, daughter or other relative of an alumnus or alumna of the college to which you are applying. At many of America's colleges and universities, legatees automatically have preference in the admissions process. Their applications are evaluated separately, and their chances of admission are greater—often far greater—than nonlegatees. Many schools in the most competitive categories offer legatees a 50–50 chance of admission, while nonlegatees have only one chance in eight, 10 or 12. The rate of admission for children of alumni in a recent Yale freshman class, for example, was 39 percent, or more than twice the 18.4 percent rate of admission for most other applicants. What this means is that if you are a nonlegatee and you are competing with a legatee with identical qualifications for the last place in the incoming freshman class, the legatee will most likely get that spot.

Not fair? Probably not. But most colleges believe in encouraging a sense of tradition among their graduates. Moreover, all colleges need the financial and moral support of their alumni. Even the most expensive colleges in America depend on contributions from alumni and other donors to cover as much as 70 percent of their operating costs. Although the costliest colleges now charge between $20,000 and $30,000 or more for tuition, fees, room, board and expenses, it actually costs them $50,000 or more to house, feed and educate each student. The deficit is covered by contributions from alumni and friends. One way of

Fox Lane High School

Class of 1994

P.O. Box 390
South Bedford Road
Bedford, NY 10506
(914) 241-6170

One-Half Mile East of
I-684 on Route 172

CEEB Code 333245

Dr. Bruce L. Dennis
Superintendent

Richard M. Kraemer
Principal

Achievement Test Means
June, 1993

English	532	N = 78
Math I	586	N = 71
Biology	592	N = 61
Chemistry	588	N = 8
Amer. History	515	N = 12
French	568	N = 6
Spanish	579	N = 15

Cumulative Range: Class of 1994

Rank in Deciles	Range of Averages
First	97.21-90.33
Second	90.30-87.44
Third	87.30-84.68
Fourth	84.61-83.02
Fifth	82.93-80.29
Sixth	80.22-78.17
Seventh	78.16-74.65
Eighth	74.46-72.25
Ninth	72.24-67.55
Tenth	67.50-

The Class of 1993 Placement

Size	196
4 Year College	69%
S.U.N.Y.	10%
N.Y. State Independent	16%
Out-of-State Public	13%
Out-of-State Private	30%
2 Year College	23%
S.U.N.Y.	18%
N.Y. State Independent	2.5%
Out-of-State	2.5%
Work	6%
Military	1%
Other	.5%
Merit Finalists	5
Letters of Commendation	14

The Class of 1994
Test Scores
PSAT/NMSQT
192 Juniors, October 1992

	Verbal	Math
75-80	0	2
70-74	5	10
65-69	4	7
60-64	6	11
55-59	10	23
50-54	23	20
45-49	21	23
40-44	35	26
35-39	28	20
30-34	17	20
25-29	24	24
20-24	19	6

Means: V = 41   M = 45

Merit Semi-Finalists................5
Letters of Commendation.........13

Scholastic Aptitude Test
134 Juniors — Spring 1993

	Verbal	Math
750-800	0	2
700-749	5	5
650-699	3	13
600-649	7	11
550-599	13	26
500-549	21	19
450-499	25	14
400-449	16	22
350-399	19	19
300-349	17	7
Below	8	6

Means: V = 455   M = 513

Figure 2   *A profile of a recent graduating class from a public school in a suburb of New York City. Such profiles are sent to college admissions offices each year to give them a better idea of how each high school ranks nationally in terms of SAT I and SAT II scores and college placement success. A profile of your school can give you a better idea of how you would rank*

Student Services

Director.............................Claire D. Friedlander
School Counselors:......Anthony Dovi, Gary Gilmore,
Ed Krupman, Susan Smith,
Carolyn Wade
Counselor Intern.......................Amanda Costin

The Community

The Fox Lane High School is located in the Town of Bedford in Northern Westchester County. The school district includes the communities of Bedford, Mt. Kisco, Bedford Hills and Pound Ridge. These are suburban commuter towns, mostly residential, with a few light industries. The socio-economic diversity of these communities is reflected in the student body.

The School

Fox Lane is a public comprehensive Senior High School of about 850 students in grades 9-12. Almost all of the 104 faculty members hold advanced degrees.

To meet the needs of all students, the program provides for four broad groupings: Honors and AP Courses, N.Y. State Regents Level Courses, General Courses, and Modified Academics. These are not tracks since a student may be in one group for some subjects and another for others. Honors sections available to the Class of '94 are English 1H, 2H, 3H, Social Studies 1H and 2H, and Math 9H 10H, and 11H.

AP Courses are available in English, American History, Calculus AB and BC, Computer Science, Physics, Chemistry, Biology, Studio Art, French, Spanish, a second college level course in Earth Science, and Music Theory.

In addition to five full-time guidance counselors, the high school has psychologists, school social workers, a speech and language clinician, a student assistance counselor, school nurse, reading and learning specialists, special educators and consultant psychiatric services.

Fox Lane is accredited by the State University of New York and by the Middle States Association of Schools and Colleges.

Marking System

Grades are given on a 0-100 basis. Four quarterly grades and a final exam are added and divided by 5 to determine a final average. The transcript shows final grades, final examination grades and/or Regents examination grades. The passing grade is 65 and the college recommending grade is 65.

Class Rank Policy

The Board of Education has abolished published Class Rank. All final grades up to the beginning of Senior Year are averaged to determine G.P.A. The cumulative range of G.P.A.'s is provided, in deciles, on the reverse side of this profile for the Class of '94.

ALL GRADES ARE UNWEIGHTED

Graduation Requirements

Both Regents and local diplomas need 20½ credits. Required credits are as follows: English — 4; Social Studies — 4; Math — 2; Science — 2; Art or Music — 1; Health — ½; Physical Education — 2. Regents Diploma candidates must have a three credit sequence in a foreign language or a five credit sequence in Art, Music or Occupational Education. Other sequences are required for both diplomas in several combinations.

Special Programs

ACES

The Academic Community for Educational Success is attended by up to 25 students each year at an off-campus site. The program features academic courses and electives, and emphasizes individual responsibility and group process. Some students from this program may choose to attend college.

Commonly Needed Transcript Interpretations

Applied Mathematics — Arithmetic courses related to technology-based employment mathematics.

Community Service — A program that allows volunteer service to community agencies; 150 hours per credit.

Earth Science 2 — A college-level geology course with labs and extensive field work culminating in the Regents College Exam in Physical Geology.

Latin 1/2 — An accelerated course that covers two years work in one.

Math 1R, 2R, 3R — NY State syllabus integrating algebra, geometry and trigonometry.

Math 4R — Pre-Calculus

Math 1, 2, 3, 4 — Non-Regents levels paralleling above courses.

Math 9H, 10H, 11H — An Honors program that prepares students for the Advanced Placement BC Course.

Modified Academics — Subjects are open only to students with identified special needs as authorized by the District Committee on Special Education.

Senior English — Most students select courses from a rigorous series of semester electives. One quarter includes Senior Composition. At least one course should be in literature.

Society, Literature and Truth — A senior level, one semester, double period, interdisciplinary course in English/Government exploring the relationships between practical efforts to build society based on shared perceptions, and the unique visions of literary artists who seek and express other levels of truth.

Across Cultures — A senior level, one semester, double period, interdisciplinary course in Economics and English which examines key issues in American society from multicultural perceptives.

Economics E/Government/Math Modules — An interdisciplinary, double period, senior level, full-year course integrating the skills and analytical tools of the three disciplines as they function for institutions and individuals in American Society.

Work Experience Program — A student may earn up to two credits in a supervised work experience program at 300 hours per credit. Included in the requirements is a classroom component. Grade: P/F

against last year's graduating class, and thus help you calculate your chances of admission to the colleges on your list. If you attend a public school, your guidance counselor has copies of your school profile. Private school profiles are compiled in **Peterson's Guide to Independent Secondary Schools,** *which you'll find in any major public library or bookstore.*

encouraging such contributions is to give children of alumni some preference in the admissions process.

The profiles and viewbooks of most colleges will tell you whether the children of alumni receive preference over nonlegatees. In the University of Michigan profile on page 00, you'll find "alumni/ae relationship" among the key elements listed under "Basis for Candidate Selection." Some colleges are forthright about legacy. Others disguise it by only saying that children of alumni are "especially encouraged to apply." If there's no such indication, you should ask the college admissions office, directly, what percentage of each freshman class consists of legatees. If 100 members of a class of 450 at a particular college are legatees, and there are 5,000 applications each year, you know that you, as a nonlegatee, will be competing with 5,000 students for only 350 open seats—not 450—and the odds of your getting in are reduced accordingly. Because of the advantages of being a legatee, it can be useful to trace your family background and see if any relatives, near or distant, dead or alive, are graduates of the colleges you'd like to apply to. Many applications ask you to list relatives who attended the college. So even a great-great-grandparent may help a little.

CONTRIBUTORS

In addition to legatees, there are other special categories of students whose individual or family backgrounds often give them an edge over other applicants. Sons or daughters of major financial contributors to almost any college or university also get special consideration for obvious reasons. There aren't too many applicants in this category, and they won't significantly reduce your chances of admission, but they will get in more easily than you and ahead of you—often with lower qualifications.

ATHLETICS

Gifted athletes also get special consideration at most colleges and universities. If the football, field hockey, basketball, baseball or any other coach says he needs some top athletes to rebuild the team, the admissions committee will keep a sharp eye out for applicants with the proper athletic qualifications. Gifted athletes can add to a college's reputation (and stadium and arena ticket sales). Unlike schools that offer athletic scholarships regardless of academic ability, most selective colleges demand that their top athletes meet all academic requirements for admission and show evidence that they'll be able to handle all college-level course work. Many selective colleges offer no "phys. ed." major, and all athletes accepted at such schools must be academically talented and qualified.

Nevertheless, many coveted athletes still get preference over nonathletes with greater academic qualifications—even at schools such as Harvard.

ACADEMICS

Academic superstars, like athletic superstars, may also receive preferential treatment by admissions committees, especially at the more prestigious colleges and universities. A mathematics wizard who may have flunked English; a gifted chemist who can't spell correctly; a published poet who flunked high school physics—all might receive preferential treatment over the more average candidate for admissions.

SPECIAL SKILLS

An applicant with special skills—a gifted musician, composer, artist, writer or actor, or any other student who will enhance the reputation of the college—will also receive preferential treatment by the admissions staff, especially if the student receives support for his application from a professor, coach, or other ranking administration or faculty member of the college. Of course, if you have a special skill, be sure to notify the college and appropriate faculty members. Just as in the case of the coach who says he needs top athletes to rebuild the team, if the conductor of the university orchestra needs a new first-oboe player, the admissions committee will keep a sharp eye out for such an applicant and give that applicant preference that other students will not get. Again, "particular talent or ability" is listed among the key elements in the college profile on page 22.

MINORITIES

Minority applicants also receive a certain degree of special consideration at many colleges and universities, and it's important for you to know how race, religion and ethnic background may affect your chances for admission at various colleges. Many parochial colleges, for example, favor members of certain religions, but others do not. Most nonsectarian schools generally try to achieve a representative mix of students by setting flexible upper and lower limits on the percentage of students they enroll from any single race or religion—regardless of whether that policy means accepting some students who may be less qualified academically than many rejected applicants. Almost all categories of colleges have at least one member of the admissions staff who specializes in the recruitment of underrepresented minorities.

GEOGRAPHY

Geography factors also affect the selection of each class at many universities, and you must take these factors into consideration in calculating your chances of admission. State universities, for example, have to give preference to applicants from their own states, because state residents pay the taxes that support such schools. Although it's difficult in many cases, most other colleges and universities—and even the state universities to some extent—try to bring together as varied a student body as possible, from many different areas and backgrounds. Again, turn to the University of Michigan profile on page 00, and you'll find "geographical distribution" listed as a key factor under "Basis for Candidate Selection."

As I pointed out in Chapter 2, there are only about three dozen nonspecialized liberal arts colleges in the top *Barron's* category of "Most Competitive" colleges—of which all but nine are in the East and too far away to make them attractive or affordable for many Westerners. It's no coincidence, therefore, that the majority of students at those colleges are Easterners. More than half the roughly 1,600 students in a recent Harvard class are from the Northeast. Only about 12 percent are from the Midwest and Plains states, about 12 percent from the South, and about 15 percent from the West (two-thirds of them from California). The remainder are from U.S. territories and from foreign countries. So, it's no coincidence either that schools outside the Northeast show some bias in favor of students from their geographic regions.

Similarly, in the second *Barron's* category of "Highly Competitive" colleges, 28 of the 64 non-specialized colleges are in the Northeast. Twenty others are in the Midwest, eight are in the South, two in Texas, six in California and the rest scattered in the West outside California. Again, those outside the Northeast show regional bias in their admissions policies. The University of Michigan at Ann Arbor insists that out-of-state applicants "must be very highly qualified." At the University of California at Berkeley, "preference for admission is always given to California residents. For California residents, if your grade-point average is 3.3 or higher...you are minimally eligible for the University." And 63 percent of the students at Trinity University in San Antonio are Texans—with good reason. After all, of the 100 nonspecialized liberal arts colleges in the two highest categories, only 16 are west of the Mississippi and most of those are in California. So, schools such as Trinity University have a right—even an obligation—to reserve most of their seats for bright local students who, for one reason or another, cannot or do not want to travel far from home to get a superior college education.

But, as in every area of the college admissions picture, geographic bias can work for or against you. As you can see from the figures above, it is more difficult for an Easterner to get into the most competitive Western colleges, and easier for a Westerner. Ironically, it is also easier for a Westerner to get into the most competitive colleges of the Northeast. That's because all of those schools are eager to achieve geographic diversity of their student bodies. Such diversity, they feel, promotes learning and, ultimately, understanding of one another. But few high school students in the West—especially in the Rocky Mountain states—ever apply, because they (and their guidance counselors) mistakenly believe that the most prestigious private colleges of the Northeast are exclusive clubs reserved primarily for wealthy students from the Northeast. Nothing could be farther from the truth. Indeed, a student from Montana, Wyoming or any other underrepresented state has a better chance of admission to schools such as Yale and Harvard than a student with identical qualifications from New York City.

THE REAL ODDS OF ADMISSION

Most of these enrollment facts and figures are available in the college profiles published either in college viewbooks or separately in the various college selection aids recommended earlier. So you should review these facts and figures to work out the realistic chances of admission before moving ahead with the application process.

Looking once again at the hypothetical college that eventually enrolls 450 freshmen out of 5,000 applicants, we know in advance that about 100 of the 450 will be legatees. Another five percent to 10 percent will probably be disadvantaged students—say 30. About five percent will be academic superstars and five percent athletic superstars—a total of 45. So 175 of the 450 have a head start in gaining admission. That leaves only 275 "open" places, of which half are for men and half for women, which leaves only 137 or 138 seats open for you and the remaining 4,825 applicants. So, the real odds of admission at such a school are not 11 to 1 (450 seats for 5,000 applicants), but 35 to 1 (275 seats for 4,825 applicants). And geographic bias could reduce those chances even further (or perhaps increase them, of course).

The point to keep in mind is that by getting a rough idea of your chances of admission to various schools in advance, you can develop a list of colleges that not only includes those you'd most like to attend, but also those where you have the greatest chances of gaining admission. That will not only save you a lot of time, energy, heartache and money, it will also assure your going to the kind of college where you'll be happy and thrive—because you know that you belong there and that they want you there. By all means apply to one or more of your dream or reach schools, even if the odds of admission seem high. You could be the one in 100 or 1,000 who gets in. But it's important for you to figure out and know those odds before you apply, to avoid a lot of hurt from unrealistic expectations.

Be certain you know what you're looking for in a college. And be certain you know what the colleges you'd like to apply to are looking for in the students they accept. Then get to work putting together an application package those colleges will find irresistible. If you do a good enough job, you may be surprised to find the top colleges competing for you!

SUMMARY

1. Grades (your high school GPA)

2. Course quality; honors and AP courses where possible

3. Class rank

4. SAT I scores (tutoring can help)

5. SAT II scores (tutoring can help)

6. AP test scores

7. Extracurricular activities

8. Out-of-school activities; summer jobs

9. Character

10. Teacher and school recommendations

11. Your application form

12. Your application essays

13. Personal interview at college and/or with alumni

14. Factors beyond your control
    a. High school quality
    b. Legacy
    c. Financial contributors
    d. Athletic and academic superstars; gifted students with special skills
    e. Minorities
    f. Geography

THE APPLICATION |4
PROCESS*|

For most students, applying to college is the first effort to emerge from the safe, secure life of home, family and friends. It's an admittedly difficult process, because it's the first time most students will have to compare themselves with other students all across the country. Until now, self-evaluation has involved the relatively simple, self-evident comparisons with people you've known intimately—brothers, sisters, relatives and friends. Until now, it has always been obvious where you've stood intellectually, socially, athletically—because you and others in your community who knew you could easily compare you with your peers. Now, for perhaps the first time in your life, total strangers are going to measure you against thousands of other students you don't know, by standards you may or may not be familiar with. It's an intimidating process, one that keeps many, many people from ever leaving home.

---

*As you'll see throughout this chapter, the ideal time to begin the application process is during your junior year in high school. If you're already a senior, you obviously have less time to work with. But, if you work quickly and carefully, it's not too late to get your application in on time. Seniors should follow each stage of the process and pay particular attention to the special time-saving tips provided throughout this chapter.

But there are millions of others such as you who do want to venture outside their home communities into a broader world, to learn from and measure themselves against others.

The college application process is much the same as the job application process, which you'll go through many times. Unfortunately, this is the first time, the most difficult and, for some, the most terrifying. You will be evaluated by people who don't know you. Then, for the first time, you will be asked to evaluate yourself—something most young people seldom have to do.

SELF-EVALUATION

Who are you? President of your class? There are class presidents in every class in every high school in America. Captain of your football team? There's a football captain, perhaps two or three, in almost every high school throughout the country. What I'm getting at is that the tallest kid on any block is seldom the tallest kid in the city, and the tallest corn stalk in any row is seldom the tallest in the field, county or state. In other words, the standards you've always used to measure yourself in your own school or community may no longer have much value or meaning when you have to measure yourself against tens of thousands of other students. What you, your family and friends rate as above average may well be rated below average in another community—and vice versa.

What will have value in the broader, more worldly sense are those qualities that make you a unique individual—and every human being is unique in some, and usually many, ways. The college application process seeks to force you, for the first time, to look at yourself, evaluate yourself and determine what makes you unique. We'll explore this in greater detail when we get to the section on writing application essays, but begin thinking about it now. It's important. It may well be that your academic skills do indeed make you unique, and that is why colleges often depend on SATs and other standardized tests, which serve as common measures of academic skills.

Another common measure they use is the application process itself, which serves to evaluate social and, to some extent, intellectual skills. Notice that I said application *process*—not just application alone. In fact, filling out the application form is just part of the application process. The rest of this chapter will discuss, in chronological order, each step you'll follow as you complete the application process: correspondence with colleges, campus visits, personal interviews, the application form, the essays, and teacher and school recommendations.

CORRESPONDENCE WITH COLLEGES

The application process begins with your first letter or postcard to colleges asking for viewbooks, brochures, course catalogs and other pertinent information. In writing for various materials, you should also ask for a profile from each college, if it is published as a separate document—although most publish all or part of it in their viewbooks. Profiles are also available in the *CADH* and *The College Handbook* (see the Summary at the end of Chapter 2). Also ask for brochures on academic subjects and athletic or extracurricular activities that are of special interest to you. Ideally, it's best to write for these materials as early as possible in your junior year so that you'll have plenty of time to decide which colleges interest you most. You shouldn't rush a decision that may affect your entire life. By taking your time, you can compare each college with the others, flipping back and forth between viewbooks and brochures, making notes, and comparing even the most minor aspects of college life. If you're already a senior, telephone for these materials to save time, or see if you can find them in your guidance counselor's office or a library.

In addition to the requested materials you'll receive, you'll also receive a flood of unsolicited materials from colleges you did not contact. That's because almost every college in the United States conducts an annual search for candidates it believes would enhance the quality of its student body. The colleges get names from computerized lists based on PSAT scores and the personal profile sheets most students fill out at the time they take their PSATs. By all means scan through the material, but get it done as soon as possible so that you narrow your list of colleges quickly.

Another reason for starting the application process early is to be first in line. Most people involved in education are fiercely proud of their institutions. Consequently, applicants who want to gain admission to selective colleges and universities must show enthusiasm and motivation. Again, applying to college is not unlike applying for a job: The person who is first in line and shows the most enthusiasm will often get the job (all other factors being equal).

So, as you go through each element of the application process, always try to be first in line and enthusiastic. Make good first impressions on everyone—from receptionists to deans of admissions.

Something to keep in mind when you write to each college is that your letter can represent an important contact with the admissions offices of those schools. Your first card or letter asking for brochures probably won't go into an application folder. Admissions offices will simply enter your name, address and high school grade level into the college computer for automatic mailings to applicants. That card or letter (or phone call, if you're a senior) should identify you as a high school student considering applying. Once in their computer data banks, you probably won't have to write again for an application, although it's always best to double-check to make certain you get applications from all colleges that interest you.

After that initial contact, any subsequent letter you write (for appointments with professors or admissions officers) will be inserted into a folder with your name; and that document could eventually become an element of your admissions package if you apply to that particular school. Admissions people often use such letters as evidence in your evaluation. They'll note the date (that's why I suggest you write early), and they'll note whether it is neatly typewritten. You should have learned by now how to type a neat business letter on either a typewriter or word processor. If you haven't, do so right away!

If You Live Overseas

If you're an American high school student living overseas, DO NOT SEND ANY CORRESPONDENCE IN BLUE AIRMAIL ENVELOPES. All mail at colleges is sorted by clerks who assume that letters in blue airmail envelopes addressed to the admissions office come from foreign students; such mail is automatically shunted to a separate and often independent office. You'll lose weeks and perhaps months writing back and forth explaining who you really are and that you're not a foreign citizen. So don't get trapped in a bureaucratic tangle. Use the same white bond stationery you'd use if you were living in the United States.

CAMPUS VISITS

The next step for you in the application process is to determine which campuses you want to visit over your winter and spring vacations. Make certain the colleges you visit are in session so you can see campus life as it will be when you attend. We discussed tours in Chapter 2, but I want to add a few more facts here. Remember, when you visit each college, the admissions office may note in your folder that you did indeed make the extra effort to tour the campus as early as you did. (Many of your high school classmates either won't bother visiting at all or will wait until summer vacation, when the college may no longer be in session.) In addition to being "first in line" once again, it's important that your dress and conduct serve you well and reflect maturity. Regardless of Hollywood portrayals of anarchic college life, in such films as *Animal House*, most campuses are relatively quiet communities for mature, hardworking students, and most admissions officers favor mature applicants who display respect for traditional standards of dress and conduct. Jeans, sneakers, gum chewing and smoking may be acceptable at some colleges after you're admitted, but they do not display maturity on a campus visit when you're only an applicant; and, like it or not, such grooming and conduct (as well as vulgar or "cool" language) may hurt your chances for admission.

Campus tours, usually conducted by student guides, give you a good opportunity to ask questions of a person who was in your shoes only a couple of years earlier. Your student guide will have experienced every fear you have and probably will know the answer to every question you can think of. So, for your own sake, don't be shy. Ask! This is the perfect time for it. And if your parents are with you, encourage them to think of and ask questions too.

Don't be surprised, by the way, if some of the members of your "tour group" include ordinary tourists. Campus tours are designed for anyone interested in seeing the college or university, and the tour groups include visitors as well as prospective applicants and their parents.

On certain days of the week—you'll have to ask in advance at each college which they are and plan accordingly— campus tours are followed by an informative lecture or question-and-answer session with an admissions office representative. Try to attend one of these in conjunction with your tour—and again, don't be shy about asking questions. Remember: There's no such thing as a silly question. If something bothers you or if you're curious about something, it's not silly. It's important, and you owe yourself an answer. These schools will charge you and your family $20,000, $25,000 or more a year. For that kind of money, they owe you the answers to any questions you may have—even the ones you think may be silly!

As I said earlier, the campus tours should allow you to reduce your list of prospective colleges to no more than eight. Upon returning home, it will be time to write or telephone for appointments for personal interviews at those colleges that still offer such interviews. Once a required element of the application process at all competitive colleges, the personal interview has now been abandoned entirely at some schools and reduced to merely a recommended procedure at others. Although it's still usually required for early-decision applicants (see page 00), few colleges require it anymore for regular-decision applicants because they simply don't have enough time or admissions officers to interview individually the thousands of students who apply each year. In addition, too many students live too far away to afford to visit the campus of each school they apply to.

At colleges that still recommend personal interviews (they'll say so in their viewbooks), I strongly recommend asking for one. Not only is it an opportunity for you to get to know more about such colleges, it could prove the critical factor in your application by allowing you to display unique qualities not evident in the dry statistics of your application and high school transcript. In other words, an interview might be an opportunity to "sell" yourself at a school where your application alone might not merit special attention. Like the personal essay, the personal interview is one of the few elements of the application process that is something you can control.

In addition, the desire and motivation exhibited by the effort to have an interview adds one more element to your package and may put you ahead of students who do not bother to have interviews because they're not required. Even at colleges that no longer grant personal interviews with admissions officers, it's important that you have a personal interview with a faculty member (preferably the department chairman) or coach in an area in which you are gifted and have demonstrated exceptional talents and skills. A recommendation from such a faculty member or coach could be critical in winning acceptance to a competitive college.

Not all colleges begin scheduling personal interviews at the same time each year. It's important to know this before writing. By late spring, most have started interviewing, however, and once again, it's a big plus for you to be first in line. It shows eagerness and desire. Even more important, though, being first in line will give you a better choice of dates and times, because few other applicants bother asking for interviews so early. Moreover, your interviewer will be able to spend more time getting to know you. An interviewer who can spend 30 to 45 minutes with each of three applicants on a relaxed summer day will remember each of them far better than he will the 16 applicants he sees on a busy day when he has to limit each interview to 15 or 20 minutes. Remember: The longer the interview, the more time you have to sell yourself. (If you're already in your senior year and don't have the time to make separate visits, I suggest you combine the campus tour and personal interview into one trip.)

Your letter requesting an interview should be neatly typed, and should mention that your decision to ask for the interview and to apply to the college was based on your tour of the campus and a careful reading of the viewbook. The aim of the letter is not only to obtain an appointment, but to display your deep interest in that particular college. Your letter should also mention any special academic, athletic or extracurricular interest you may have, and should request an interview (in addition to the admissions office interview) with a professor, coach or other college staff member specializing in any of those areas. (You may want to write directly to such professors or coaches for special interviews, if you know their names.) Request such special interviews only if you've demonstrated special skills and talents. If you're only vaguely interested in a special area, you'll be able to learn all about it in the admissions office interview.

In your letter you may also want to ask for the opportunity to attend one or more classes in areas that interest you, but, in planning your trip to each college, remember to allow enough time at each campus to do all the things you want to accomplish. You'll have to allow, for example, at least one full day (perhaps even a day and a half) at any campus where you want to combine a tour, personal interview, special interview and visit to a class or two.

If you live too far away to afford a visit to some of the colleges you'd like to apply to, there are alternatives to on-campus tours and personal interviews. Representatives of most major colleges and universities make regular annual visits to various high schools and communities, where they show videos of their campuses, describe and explain their colleges, and answer questions. Some also conduct personal interviews, although personal interviews are just as often handled by local alumni volunteers. You can arrange such an interview by writing or calling the admissions office.

These substitutes for actual campus visits are perfectly acceptable to most colleges, because few require such visits. But I think such substitutes do the applicant a disservice. No campus representatives, and few alumni, will tell you the negative aspects of their college. The only way to learn enough about a college—enough to decide whether you want to spend four years there—is to visit personally. I can't urge you strongly enough to do just that. If at all possible, you should sleep overnight with students in the dorms. Most major colleges provide student hosts and arrange such over-night visits if you write to the admissions office in advance. Again, this kind of enthusiasm and determination displays maturity that will work in your favor in the application process.

You may want to visit some campuses twice (once for a tour and personal interview, and again for an overnight stay)—if you plan to be a serious candidate at the most competitive colleges. Unless you're an athletic, academic or other form of superstar with sterling credentials, you'll have to show a lot of evidence of desire and motivation (in addition to good grades and all the other qualifications) to gainadmissiontoacompetitivecollege.Remember, you can take the campus tour on the day of your personal interview; but if it's midsummer, some colleges may be out of session, and you won't be able to visit classes, talk to undergraduates and see student life in action. That's why I suggest that juniors visit campuses in winter or spring and make a second visit for personal interviews in summer. By visiting when college is in session, you may decide against applying and can therefore dispense with the interview and application. (Incidentally, do not confuse a personal interview with the group meetings for prospective applicants that admissions officers routinely schedule on college campuses and often in various high schools in the fall. Although they willingly answer all questions at such sessions, that is not the same as a personal interview, which is an extended, one-to-one private meeting with a representative of the admissions office.)

THE PERSONAL INTERVIEW

Regardless of who interviews you—an admissions officer, alumnus, coach or professor—the same rules and techniques apply. In fact, you'll be able to use the techniques discussed below in interviews for the rest of your life. Once again, remember that the interview is one of the two elements in the application process that is almost totally under your control. Both in the college application process and later on in life, an interview is an opportunity for you to display those aspects of your personality that may not show up in the dry statistics of an application. Before discussing the interview itself, it's important to remember that whoever interviews you will note your appearance and conduct. Parents often bore you with admonitions to "sit up straight," "look at me when I talk to you" or "comb your hair." I'm sure you've heard it all. But any applicant who wants serious consideration at a selective college or university should, for once, pay heed to those parental commands. For they are nothing more than adult standards, and the college representative who interviews you is an adult who is only interested in admitting adults to college or university. True, admissions officers understand kids— and like them—but they simply will not admit them to university.

So, if you're not interested in adhering to such standards, decide that in advance and don't waste your time and money by traveling to the college interview.

A few years ago, the director of admissions at a prestigious Eastern college regretfully rejected one of the best candidates applying for admission that year. The son of one of the college's most loyal and generous alumni, the applicant had been tops in his high school class academically and athletically. But he arrived for his college interview with an open-necked sports shirt, blue jeans and sneakers—with no socks. When asked to sit down, he promptly put his feet on the desk!

"He was still a rebellious adolescent," explained the admissions director, "and we didn't think he was ready for our college—despite his obvious talents and abilities. We insist on maturity as well as talent."

Figures 3 and 4 show interviewer reactions to two candidates. One was rejected, the other accepted by a highly competitive college. Note that the interviewer rates each candidate for appearance, conversational ability, attitude toward school and society generally, previous successes, and attractiveness as a candidate for the college. The interviewer is then asked to recommend accepting, rejecting or wait-listing the candidate. (Wait-listing is discussed in Chapter 6.)

Aside from proper dress, conduct and manners, proper language could well be a decisive factor in your interview. The repetitive use of the word "like" and the phrase, "ya know," as in "Like . . . ya know . . ." will certainly elicit negative reactions from interviewers. So will responses such as "Cool!" and immature speech patterns, such as, "Well, ya know, I kinda like history, ya know, and then, well, English, ya know, and, ya know . . ." Rude one-word answers will also leave your interviewer unimpressed and hurt your chances of admission—as they did the student whose interview began this way:

Interviewer: How was your trip here?
Student applicant: Good.
Interviewer: Did you come by car?
Student applicant: Yeah.
Interviewer: Well, how's school going this year?
Student applicant: Good.

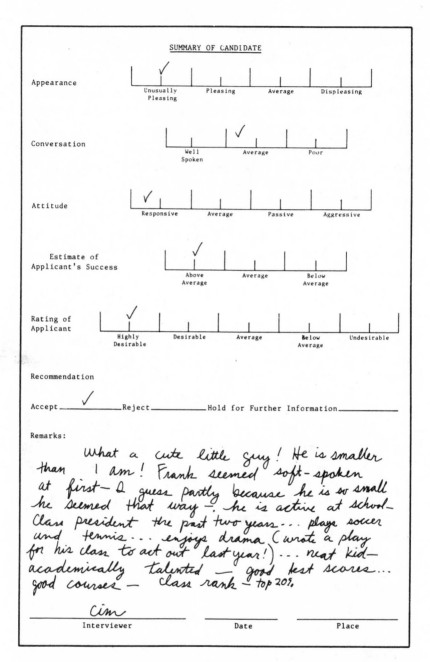

SUMMARY OF CANDIDATE

Appearance
Unusually Pleasing — Pleasing — Average — Displeasing

Conversation
Well Spoken — Average — Poor

Attitude
Responsive — Average — Passive — Aggressive

Estimate of Applicant's Success
Above Average — Average — Below Average

Rating of Applicant
Highly Desirable — Desirable — Average — Below Average — Undesirable

Recommendation

Accept ___✓___ Reject _____ Hold for Further Information _____

Remarks:

What a cute little guy! He is smaller than I am! Frank seemed soft-spoken at first — I guess partly because he is so small he seemed that way — he is active at school — Class president the past two years... plays soccer and tennis... enjoys drama (wrote a play for his class to act out last year!)... neat kid — academically talented — good test scores... good courses — class rank — top 20%.

Cim

_____   _____   _____
Interviewer   Date   Place

Figures 3 and 4 *Here are the actual interview forms, along with the interviewer's appraisals, notes and recommendations, from personal interviews conducted at a highly selective, private four-year college. Appearance,*

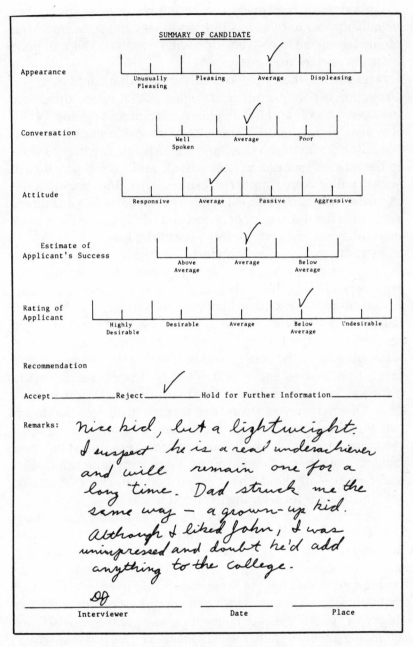

conversational ability and attitude are the first things judged in every college interview.

Although such answers can be the result of shyness, they usually appear to others as unfriendliness and rudeness. Your ability to engage in conversation will be seen as a sign of good manners and friendliness.

And still another error in the interview that could earn you a rejection is poor grammar. If you do not know the difference between "good" and "well," learn it! "School is going WELL this year"—not "good"! That's seventh grade grammar, as is the difference between "me" and "I." "Me and my friends went to the movies" should be "My friends and I went . . ." If such speech patterns are simply the result of bad habits, begin changing those habits in your everyday speech early in your junior year. Such habits may not only cost you admission to the college of your choice, they may affect your entire life.

In addition to proper conduct, it's important to go into a personal interview knowing as much about the particular college as possible. When asked why you're interested in a particular college—and many interviewers will ask you that—you should know why specifically, on the basis of your in-depth reading about the academic, athletic, social and other opportunities offered by the college and outlined in its viewbooks and brochures. Just as every individual is unique, so are many colleges and universities—especially the most competitive ones. One may have a strong department in an area that interests you, or a particular professor whose books you've read. Whatever it is, study of the college brochures, viewbook and catalog, your tour of the campus, talks with undergraduates and faculty—all should have given you a number of strong, specific reasons for wanting to attend that school.

The interview will, of course, cover far more ground than that, but you must be prepared to answer that basic question—not only for the college representative, but also for yourself. If you don't know why you want to go to a particular college perhaps you don't belong there and should not apply. The fact that your friends are going is not a good reason! Nor is the fact that it's a "great" college. There are many great colleges. Once again, we get back to that word *unique*. You've got to discover what makes each college unique and why you want to go to that particular college.

The personal interview is another common measuring stick that colleges can use to compare students of different backgrounds from all parts of the country. Whether you're shy or outgoing, the interview is something you'll have to face all your life. It is a universal measuring device. A good way to get used to it is to rehearse with parents. Have them ask you questions, and then answer them as completely as possible. Rehearse your entrance: walking into the interviewer's office with quiet self-confidence, smiling and looking him or her straight in the eye and shaking hands firmly. Rehearse your exit: shaking hands again, thanking him or her for the interview, then turning and walking out—again with quiet self-confidence. Your appearance, language, bearing and conduct will all go down in the interviewer's notes. So, it's important to rehearse often. Move the furniture around at home to devise a stage set—with a desk or table in the middle; you on one side; your mother or father on the other. When you're good at it at home, use an interview at one of your safety schools as a "dress rehearsal" (although don't let them know that!).

Interview techniques vary from college to college and from person to person. Most college admissions officers are genuinely warm and exceptionally skilled interviewers, and their first questions are generally random ones aimed at putting you at ease and hitting on some topic that will get you talking comfortably. The interviewer is trying to get an idea of your personality and the way you think by your ability to speak, handle questions and conduct a mature discussion. He will not be asking any "loaded" questions. There won't be any "right" or "wrong" answers.

It's important, though, to be prepared for the unexpected. One interviewer I once knew invited applicants to sit down— and then he sat in silence staring at them, waiting for them to say something first. Although most interviewers are not that cruel, the best way to avoid such devastating surprises is to have endless rehearsals. As you rehearse, though, keep in mind the original meaning of the word *interview*. Most people use it to mean one person questioning another, but the original meaning is to "see one another"—in other words, for *two* people to see each other—not one to see the other.

So an interview should be a two-way exchange. In other words, there are two reasons for you to go to interviews— for college representatives to get to know you and for you to get to know them, or at least the organizations they represent, i.e., their colleges. There is nothing wrong, for example, in asking interviewers about their own experiences at college and how things may have changed since they attended. Even in the face of the unlikely silent interviewer, you should be prepared to open the conversation by thanking him for seeing you and then explaining why you came, i.e., to tell him something about yourself and to ask some questions about the college.

"Do you have any questions?" is a question even the most unskilled interviewer will almost always ask. (Not every admissions officer is a cool veteran. For some, it may be the first day on the job and you their first interviewee. The interviewer may be as nervous as you, and you may have to carry the load of the interview!) And you should indeed have some questions to ask. In fact, many of the colleges that no longer require or even conduct traditional personal interviews will grant appointments to answer applicants' questions. As I mentioned before, one important question to ask before you and your family consider spending $25,000 or more a year at any college is the percentage of undergraduate courses taught by teaching assistants (TAs) instead of senior faculty (see page 26). Remember, if you're paying for the best, you have a right to expect it.

College brochures and viewbooks can't possibly answer every question you'll have about the next four, incredibly important years of your life. So it's up to you to get those answers now—before you invest your time and money in a college. Even if you have no original questions, at least be prepared to ask the interviewer to clarify or confirm some of the many things you've read about the college or heard from some of your friends or advisers.

More important than "intelligent" questions that you ask will be the answers you give to the questions the interviewer will ask you directly or indirectly. By the time you walk into your first interview you should be prepared to display those elements of your character, background and skills that make you a desirable, unique applicant.

In response to the vaguest of interview questions, such as "Tell me about yourself," you should be prepared to outline the highlights of your life: school grades (have copies of your first three years' grades to show); approximate class rank; major athletic and extracurricular achievements; quick summary of family life, including an indication of financial circumstances, religious affiliation (if it's important in your life) or minority status (if it's not immediately evident and if it's important in your life); outside activities, such as job and travel; and, finally, those aspects that make you a unique individual.

What Makes You Uniquely You

By now you should have discovered, through careful and thorough self-evaluation, some of the things that make you unique: your unusual summer job; your work as a volunteer; your financial contributions to your family; the physical or mental handicaps you've overcome; your handling of your parents' divorce problems or the death of a parent; the story of how you were adopted; the deep study you've made of your interest or hobby; your work with migrant workers' children; the way you helped deliver a newborn animal (or maybe even a human baby); how you made your own incubator and hatched live chicks, or nurtured other animals; your reaction to a travel experience, or to current events at home, or in national or international affairs; what you've learned from a personal romance or from working in a political campaign; how you started a successful business; how a good deed or bad deed affected your life and taught you an important lesson; how something you studied or read or did in school affected your life....

You could go on and on thinking of the things that make you unique. Try making a list. Just restudy the characters you've read about in literature, everyone from Huck Finn to Romeo or Juliet, and you'll realize the reason we all remember such characters is because they are unique. As you list the things that make them unique, you'll begin to understand how every individual is unique—as you are. The interviewer will want to know what makes you unique so that he can see what makes you different from and more desirable than other applicants. It's here that most otherwise exceptional applicants fail most frequently—by merely reciting the list of their academic, artistic, musical and athletic achievements, their class officerships and team captaincies—while neglecting to present themselves as unique individuals.

Courage, deep love and caring for others, patriotism, profound involvements are all qualities that make various individuals unique. Harvard and Radcliffe colleges put it this way in one viewbook:

> We are keenly interested in attracting and admitting candidates who not only give ample proof of academic prowess, but also show evidence of such personal qualities as honesty, fairness, compassion, altruism, leadership, and initiative in their high school years.
>
> In addition to artistic, athletic, extracurricular, and academic talent, we recognize in the admissions process the development of strong personal qualities.

Before you go into any interview, you should have all the elements of your life detailed in your mind and ready to discuss in any order, either in piecemeal answers to many questions or in an interesting discourse in answer to a single, general question. And don't be afraid to bring notes with you; it's perfectly acceptable to refer to them during the interview. Know them by heart, of course, but don't be afraid to pause and look at them and say, "I just want to make sure I've covered everything." Notes are also handy for questioning your interviewer. Again, don't be afraid to say, "Yes, I wrote a few questions down," and then look at your notes.

Most thoughtful interviewers will ask you whether there's anything you'd like to tell them about yourself that they may not have asked; but don't risk their forgetting to do so. You must be your own advocate in an interview. It's up to you to display your strengths, so don't dwell too long on some unimportant aspect of your life while forgetting to talk about your strong points. *Make sure you get to these as early in your interview as possible.* In recounting your strong points, however, it's important that you do so with a sense of modesty and objectivity so that you do not sound overbearing or pompous.

Your Weak Points

One other important area to discuss about yourself in any interview is your weak points. Nobody's perfect, and you'll certainly leave the interviewer with a negative impression if you do not or cannot discuss your weak points. By raising them yourself in the course of the discussion, you not only show maturity, you can actually offset or at least cushion their effects on your candidacy. Remember that on paper, weaknesses and strengths all seem to weigh the same. For example, a year of bad grades in ninth grade would seem to balance a year of good grades in tenth—on paper. The interview situation, however, gives you a chance to explain your weak performance. Perhaps you had just moved from your old home, for example, and were having adjustment problems—quite normal for a 14-year-old, and probably enough for an admissions officer to make a note in your folder to ignore that one weak year if every subsequent year has been strong.

Don't, however, discuss your personal or emotional problems. The college representative is not a psychoanalyst. *Discuss only those weaknesses that will ultimately appear in your application package in one form or another and possibly affect your chances of admission.* It's to your advantage to bring up your weak points in the course of your interview to see if and how they'll affect your chances of acceptance. (Be sure to bring them up during—not at the end of—your interview. In fact, you should never end—or begin—an interview on a negative note. Be sure to make a good first impression as well as leave a good final impression on the mind of your interviewer.)

Occasionally, it's even possible to convert what would certainly appear to be weak points on paper into strong ones, if they're explained carefully. Here is an example:

> A student with lower-than-average combined SAT scores pointed out to his interviewers (in advance of filing his application) that he had never scored well in timed, instant-response tests, including IQ tests. He admitted his problem with such tests, but said he did not feel they reflected his ability to perform academically at a superior level. He backed up his contention by showing each interviewer copies he had made of his freshman-, sophomore- and junior-year transcripts, which showed him to be a consistent honors and often high-honors student. He also scored 4s (next to the highest level nationally) in AP tests at the end of his junior year. (That's why I urged you before to take AP courses in your junior year, if you're eligible, so that the test scores can influence your chances of admission if they're high enough.)

By laying his cards on the table at the interviews and tackling one of his own negative qualities head on, he not only impressed interviewers by his display of maturity, he persuaded them to place less value on his SAT scores in measuring his academic abilities. The interview thus provided him with an opportunity to discuss the extenuating circumstances of the negative elements in his package, and the colleges ignored those weak points in their final decisions.

So you must not give up on yourself or your chances simply because of weaknesses in one or more areas. Look to your strengths, not your weaknesses, as gauges of your chances for admission. If at all possible, use the interview as an opportunity to display those strengths and bring out that little spark that makes you a special person. Don't be afraid to admit that you have some weaknesses—that's only human—but make certain you can define your strengths and the characteristics that make you as unique as the student I've described above.

If the colleges you apply to do not grant personal interviews of any kind, you'll then have to rely on your application essay, and the report and recommendations from your school officials to display the qualities that make you unique.

In addition to your background, most interviewers will also want to determine the depth of your intellect. So be prepared for such questions as "What kinds of books not required by your school have you read lately?" or "What do you think about [some major current event]?" If you plan to apply to a highly selective school, you'd better have read some books outside of school, and be up-to-date on and have some opinions and understanding about current events. If you've been lazy about such things, start making up for it immediately. Read the newspaper regularly. Get a subscription to a weekly news magazine such as *Newsweek* or *Time*, or read the library copy regularly each week. Watching TV news is not enough! Ask your librarian or your teachers to suggest some good books on subjects that interest you—astronomy, for example, or art or travel. If you prefer fiction, discuss with your English teacher the type of fiction you most enjoy, and ask for suggestions of current or past novels. Whatever you do, don't reach for cheap romance novels or thrillers off the racks in your local drugstore or supermarket. Remember, as you prepare for your interview you'll be meeting with a college or university graduate—an educated, cultured individual. You must show yourself to be an educated, cultured individual too.

The Interview Commitment

There is one other great value of an interview with admissions officers, if you can arrange one—especially a longer, more relaxed one in summer. By allowing interviewers to get to know all about you, they may then be in a position to give you the broad odds of your being admitted. No admissions officers will give you a firm commitment on the basis of an interview, of course, nor can they. After all, they have no way of knowing the quality of all the other applicants with whom you'll eventually be compared. No matter how outstanding a candidate you may be, there's simply no way to know where you'll rank among other candidates in any given year. It's perfectly possible for any candidate for a competitive college to have ranked among the best applicants in last year's class and far lower this year. So it would be rude to demand a status report from admissions officers before they have been able to compare you with all other applicants. But if you've given them a chance to get to know you well—if you've truly leveled with them—there's no reason you cannot ask politely whether they think you're the kind of student the college generally accepts. Or, putting the question another way, you may ask whether they think it would be worthwhile for you to pursue your application.

If they strongly urge you to apply elsewhere, explaining that your candidacy is weak in comparison to most applicants in the past, that's certainly a strong indication that your chances of admission are poor. If they tell you to apply elsewhere but say that your qualifications match those of most students at the college or are superior, then your chances are decent to good. In some rare cases, an admissions representative may actually recruit you actively and urge you to apply for early decision (see page 118). That, of course, would be an indication that you're virtually "in."

More than likely, if you've done a good job of preinterview research, the admissions representative will tell you that your record indicates that you could do the work at that college, but that you'd better show some improvement in your weakest areas—in a particular subject, for example, or in your SATs.

Here are two other things to keep in mind during your interview. First, try not to think of your interviewer or any other admissions officer as someone who is trying to keep you or any other applicant out of college. Admissions officers are recruiters, not gatekeepers, and they are deeply concerned that the applicants they recruit are right for their colleges and that their colleges are right for the students who eventually enroll— and that means you. In other words, interviewers are not adversaries; they are men and women working for the best interests of their colleges and universities and the students who attend those schools.

With that in mind, here is a second tip for your interview. No admissions officer wants to feel his college is your safety school. So take the attitude that, for now, all the colleges on your list are first choices until you've seen them all. In other words, be open-minded and enthusiastic.

As you leave, the interviewer might ask whether you've come by yourself. If you're with one or both of your parents, be certain to introduce them cordially. Rehearse this at home if necessary. Don't just say, "This is my father." Say, "Mr. Jones, I'd like you to meet my father, Mr. Smith. Dad, this is Mr. Jones, the assistant dean of admissions." As likely as not, your interviewer may ask you to invite your parents into his office for a short conversation after your interview—to see if they have any questions. Or he may simply sit down with them in the reception room and chat for a while.

Sometimes your interviewer will come to the reception area to receive you instead of asking the receptionist to send you to his or her office. In that case, you'll have to introduce your parent or parents first. Usually the interviewer will take control of the situation after a few introductions and some small talk by saying to your parents, "Will you please excuse us while I have a chat with your [son or daughter] in my office, and perhaps you'd like to join us a little later so that I can answer your questions."

To hedge against the possibility that the interviewer fails to make it clear that your parents are not welcome at *your* interview, be certain that your parents know in advance that the admissions interview is a strictly private one between student and interviewer. Parents are not welcome, and can damage a student's chance of admission if they don't wait until they are personally *invited* to join the interviewer. Here, for example, are one admission officer's notes from an interview at which the student's mother refused to be separated from her daughter and forced her way in: "Very pleasant young lady, but Mom did most of the talking. I'm concerned about her [the student's] verbal skills, because she never really said much." The student was not admitted to that college.

Before leaving, remember to get the interviewer's full name and title (ask for a business card)—so that you can write a letter of thanks for his or her taking the time to see you and give you so much information about the college.

One final word about manners: There is nothing more irritating to most interviewers than the discovery, after spending a half-hour or more with an applicant, that the young man or woman doesn't even know the interviewer's name. Some interviewers, as they say good-bye to an applicant, purposely add, "If you think of any more questions, write to me, and I'll answer them. You have my name, don't you?"

That embarrassing last confrontation can destroy the value of an otherwise perfect interview. So, know and remember the interviewer's name *before* you enter his or her office, and use it from time to time in the interview. Be certain to use interviewer names in greeting and bidding them good-bye. Again, it's a sign of maturity that is almost always noted. Within a week after each interview, it's important to send a neatly typed thank-you note.

Special Interviews

While visiting each college, you should—if you're exceptionally talented in academics, athletics, music, dance, acting, art, writing, etc.—also request a personal interview with the appropriate professor or coach in the area in which you excel. Even if the college does not grant personal interviews with admissions office personnel, you should arrange for such special faculty interviews. The best way to arrange such special interviews is to write directly to the professor or coach for an appointment. Under no circumstances should your parents write. Either you or *the appropriate member of your high school faculty* should write such a letter and either cite or enclose documentation attesting to your accomplishments. If your credentials are strong enough, the professor or coach may well contact the admissions department on behalf of your application.

A strong positive word to admissions from either a professor or coach can push your package out of the ordinary pile into the pile for exceptional applicants and thus increase (sometimes even assure) your chances of admission. At some of the most competitive colleges, your chances of admission as an academic, artistic or athletic superstar can rise to as much as one in two instead of the usual one in eight for most applicants. At some exceptionally athletics-oriented schools, your talents may earn you an on-the-spot admissions offer and perhaps even a scholarship. As with the admissions office interviewer, be certain to get your special-interest interviewer's full name and address (ask for a business card) and send him or her a thank-you letter as soon as you return home.

Alumni Interviews

Whether you have an on-campus interview or not, some colleges and universities may require an interview with an alumnus who lives in or near your community. Alumni usually conduct interviews at their homes or offices. The special alumni interviews often serve as substitutes for on-campus interviews at colleges whose admissions offices can no longer cope with the crush of applicants or as an alternative for students who live too far away to make campus visits.

Alumni interviews can be somewhat different from those with admissions officers because most alumni have less experience dealing with high school students. For them, interviewing applicants is not a profession. It is an avocation. Most are successful business or professional leaders with a deep, abiding love for their former colleges and universities, and a willingness to work for and contribute time and money to those institutions. In other words, they have a desire to serve their old alma maters. Theirs is an emotional, rather than academic commitment, and you should demonstrate considerable enthusiasm to impress them. Alumni interviews probably cannot help your application as much as on-campus interviews with admissions officers or faculty members, but they might hurt you if you leave a negative impression with your interviewer. So treat them seriously.

Most alumni interviewers have been instructed by their colleges to try to determine the same things about the applicants they interview. The alumni you meet, therefore, will try to learn about your special attributes, your particular accomplishments, your capacity for leadership, your level of maturity, your goals, what's important to you, what motivates you and what you can contribute to the particular college. They'll want to see if you have a sense of humor and whether you can communicate well with others. And, they'll want to see how articulate you are— whether you speak like a cultured adult!

In discussing your chances of admission with alumni interviewers (and even with faculty interviewers), remember that they are almost never in a position to assure you admission. Only a member of the admissions committee can do that. So don't get your hopes too high after a successful alumni interview—even if you're told that you'll probably get in, alumni simply do not and cannot know the number and quality of applicants you're competing with.

THE APPLICATION

Your interviews and campus visits should help you reduce to no more than eight (and preferably four to six) the number of colleges and universities to which you will actually apply. You should spend the rest of the summer between junior and senior year filling in application forms and preparing the best essays you've ever written in your life. At the time of your visits to admissions offices, pick up spare out-of-date applications for practice, and make certain your name is on the mailing list of each college to receive the new application forms for your class. They are usually mailed out in mid- to late summer. Because they change little from year to year, however, you'll find the applications that arrive later easier to fill in if you've already prepared the older ones in pencil as rough drafts for copying.

Some applications are simple to fill out; others are quite complex. Most applications, however, fall somewhere in between. Indeed, most are so similar that an expanding group of several hundred colleges and universities now issue a "Common Application" (see page 98), which is accepted instead of those colleges' own applications. Eventually, the vast majority of selective colleges in the United States will use the Common Application. Such prestigious institutions as Bowdoin, Bucknell, Colgate, Cornell, Duke, Harvard, Johns Hopkins, Swarthmore, Trinity, Wellesley, Wesleyan and Williams already do. You should be able to get the Common Application from your guidance counselor or college adviser.

The Common Application allows you to fill out the one form, and send photocopies to any of the participating colleges listed at the top of the application. By giving you and your teachers and your counselors who write recommendations but one form to fill out, the Common Application has eliminated hundreds of pages of useless, unnecessary and repetitive paperwork.

Indeed, the Common Application has eliminated *all* paperwork for many students, because it's also available on computer disks. So, instead of having to type out the application, you can fill out the form on computer and print it out as many times as you want, if you have the appropriate equipment. Some colleges are even accepting disks from applicants instead of making them print out the finished forms, and the College Board has developed a computerized network to permit students and high school guidance offices to file applications and high school records electronically.

By simply filling in the Common Application once on a computer (either at home or at the guidance office) you can then transmit it electronically to the College Board and, by indicating the colleges you want to apply to, have them transmit it, along with your school records, to those colleges.

Called ExPAN, the College Board's program allows you to conduct a college search, send one letter of inquiry to obtain any number of college catalogs and viewbooks, transmit a portfolio of all your high school activities and accomplishments, and, most importantly, fill out just one Common Application. The College Board and its computers will take care of the rest of the burdensome task of getting all the data to and from all the colleges.

Whether filing by computer or by mail, however, don't, under any circumstances, use the Common Application as an easy, "shotgun" application to a dozen or more schools. First of all, it's expensive, because you have to file an application fee for each college you apply to—whether you apply electronically or by mail. Secondly, it's important—indeed, it's essential—that you apply only to those colleges that are best for you and that you truly want to attend.

If you use the Common Application and want to apply for early decision or early action to any college, you'll have to attach a letter to that effect. Some participating colleges also require supplementary information, including, in some cases, an extra essay. The Common Application includes data sheets that spell out these extra requirements for each college, and those colleges will send you the extra sheet or two to fill out with the Common Application.

Using the Common Application will save you an enormous amount of paperwork. Admissions directors have assured me that they are scrupulous in showing no favoritism between their own and the Common Application. Many of the schools no longer even bother printing their own applications.

Under no circumstances should you send the Common Application to nonparticipating colleges—i.e., colleges whose names do not appear in the list on the Common Application. That does not mean you cannot use some or all of the material from the Common Application for applications to nonparticipating colleges. You certainly can. Indeed, your essay, which we'll discuss later, can be used and reused on many other applications, as can many of the answers to other questions. Be sure to type new copies of your essay, however, for each of the applications other than the Common Application.

Completing the Application

Although most of the questions are fairly obvious, let's take a close look at the Common Application beginning on page 98, which has been filled in with fictional information.

1. *Legal name:* Your legal name is the one that appears on your current birth certificate. Many people assume the name of a stepparent, but that does not make it legal unless the courts have made it so. Be consistent about your name throughout your application. If the name Eugene Everett Richards appears on the top line, it should not be changed to Eugene E. Richards or E. Eugene Richards on subsequent lines.

2. *Prefer to be called*: Next, put your nickname down if you like it and want it publicized. It probably will be publicized if you put it down, because most colleges put out a yearbook for

incoming freshmen, so that you and all your new classmates can get to know each other more quickly.

3. *Former last name(s) if any*: The question on former last names applies only to married women and to students who have made any legal changes in their names—usually because they've been adopted. The colleges need to know your previous last name to avoid confusion when they receive transcripts from earlier years with your old name on them.

4. *Are you applying as a freshman or transfer student?*: Put a check in the "freshman" box only if you've never attended college before. If you've attended college before and are transferring—even if you're going to repeat freshman year—check the box marked "transfer student."

5. *For the term beginning*: Enter the month and year you plan to enter college.

6. *Permanent home address*: Your permanent home address is where you live most of the time and where you want all your mail from college to be sent. Your legal residence may be different if your legal guardian lives elsewhere.

7. *Possible area(s) of academic concentration/major*: Limit your answer to no more than three areas. Enter one- or two-word answers only, such as "English literature" or "political science." Do not use complete sentences, such as "I am interested in American history." If you haven't decided between two or three areas, put them all down. Your answer here is *not* binding in any way.

8. *Special college or division . . .* : The question refers to special areas of concentration, such as engineering, drama, music and other fields requiring special facilities at most institutions.

9. *Possible career or professional plans*: Don't be afraid to mark "undecided"—unless, of course, you do indeed have some preferences in this area.

10. *Will you be a candidate for financial aid?*: Make certain you answer "yes" if you will need some financial aid. As I stated previously, if you're a desirable candidate, the college to which you apply will do everything possible to insure your obtaining all the financial aid you need—from a few hundred dollars to many thousands—so that you can go there.

11. *Optional items*: By all means fill in the box with optional questions (you'll find a similar one on most applications). The answers cannot hurt you. They can only help. Years ago, Ameri-

can colleges and universities openly discriminated on the basis of race, religion and national origins. Such discrimination is now not only a violation of both federal and state laws, but also a shameful embarrassment for most top-ranked colleges, who now work hard to achieve a balanced student body. Although the colleges can no longer force you to disclose such information about yourself, it may prove advantageous to you to do so if you're a member of a traditionally underrepresented group.

12. *Educational data*: Here, "School you attend now" refers only to high school, 9th through 12th grades. The date of your graduation will probably be in June of your senior year. Be certain you enter the correct year. After the name of the school you now attend, put the ACT/CEEB code number, a six-digit number that makes it easier for computers used by the American College Testing Program and College Entrance Examination Board to identify your school when scoring your ACT and SAT tests. You'll find the number listed in either the ACT or CEEB booklets, or your guidance counselor can provide you with it.

13. *Other secondary schools*: Here you must name any other high schools that you've attended since ninth grade (in chronological order), regardless of the reasons for such attendance. The information is on your transcripts, so you must list them. The listing must include summer schools.

14. *List all college courses*: Although primarily for students transferring from other colleges, this listing gives you an opportunity to list any courses you may have taken at a college in some sort of advanced studies program for high school students. You must, however, have taken such courses for actual college credits, and you must call or write to the registrar's office of the college to send you a transcript for copying and enclosure with each college application. Under *Degree Candidate?*, which again is for transfer students, write "no" if you took the course while still in high school.

15. *If not currently attending school . . .* : If, for one reason or another, you're not in school, you must check the box on this item and write a short essay to *describe in detail* why and what you've done with your time. It may be that you graduated early; it may be that you graduated from high school a year ago, not planning to go to college, but have since changed your mind. Regardless of why, you must explain the situation and detail

what you've done between then and now. If you've just fooled around doing nothing, your chances of acceptance by a competitive college might go down. But if you've led a productive life, your chances of acceptance will be unaffected and might even go up, depending on what you've been doing.

16. *Test information*: Simply list the dates you have taken or plan to take the SATs or ACTs. List the subjects of the SAT II tests you plan taking—American history, for example, or French. Remember: You must take the SAT I and SAT II tests by the end of your junior year to apply for early decision, so that the scores are reported to the colleges by the October 1–November 1 deadlines for most such applications.

17. *Family*: Unless you have been adopted, list your actual birth mother and father under these categories—not a stepparent. If a stepparent has become your legal guardian, however, you may want to write that stepparent's name beneath your mother's or father's name and identify it by noting, "Legal guardian: [name], stepfather [or stepmother or foster father or mother]".

Under parent occupations, it is acceptable to write "Housewife" or "Deceased," if either applies. Write "Self-Employed" and the type of work (business consultant, carpenter, etc.), if your parent works for himself or herself and not for a specific company or organization. After *Name of college* and *Name of professional or graduate school*, you must list two-year or four-year colleges and graduate schools of *accredited* colleges and universities, as listed in *Barron's*. Simply write "none," if that's the case. It will have no bearing on your application. Do not list commercial trade schools. The same applies to colleges and degrees of your brothers and sisters.

18. *Academic honors*: Use short, one- or two-word answers to list all awards and distinctions *relating to schoolwork only*. This does not include such things as election as a class officer or starring in the school play or winning a good conduct award as the student who has contributed most to the school. *Academic* implies school work, and if you misinterpret such questions, you're risking a negative response to your application. You must answer questions correctly and follow directions. List academic honors chronologically, starting with ninth grade. List such things as: Ninth Grade Science Award for highest grades in general science; Tenth Grade History Award; Dean's List (honors), 9th, 10th, 11th grades; High Honors, 11th grade.

19. *Extracurricular and personal activities*: This section gives you the chance to tell about all your other contributions to school, community and family life, as well as your hobbies and other outside interests. Notice that they ask you to list them in the order of interest to you. Be realistic in doing so. Don't, in other words, put school dance committee ahead of, say, a newspaper or yearbook memLership. But if, for example, a sports team captaincy is more important to you than participation on the yearbook, list the captaincy first. Go back to Chapter 3 and use some of that material as a guide in listing some of your nonscholastic activities. Without being dishonest, try to put them in an order that will most impress college admissions officials. Don't list "listening to rock music," "visiting malls" or "watching 'soaps'" as important activities. Again, use one- and two-word answers, such as "school newspaper" (under the *Activity* column) and "sports editor" (under the column marked *Positions held, honors won, or letters earned*); or "student government" in the first column, with your title—president, vice president, or even aide if you work in student government affairs but have never run for or won election to office.

Include in this section, too, all of your most interesting activities outside school—but not work activities, which go below in another section. In this section, for example, you might put travel—if you've done some unusual and extensive travel—or skiing, swimming, waterskiing, sailing and other sports in which you participate outside of school. Again, don't be dishonest and enter things you don't do, just to impress admissions people. By all means enter such activities as reading, if you spend an hour or two a day on outside reading; Bible study, if you indeed do so; and volunteer work if that too is an important outside activity. Be sure to include the fact that you play a musical instrument, but don't include the fact that you play video games (or any other games, for that matter—unless you're a Grand Master at chess!).

If you have special skills in any academic, athletic or artistic area, by all means indicate that on this (and all other) applications. List all awards or other accomplishments associated with that talent, and enclose *copies*, not originals, of your work. An athlete, for example, might enclose a videotape, along with some newspaper clippings about exceptional performances. An actor, musician or performer might do the same (and include copies of programs and playbills). But make certain any sound tapes are of professional quality, with professional introduction. One musi-

Albion • Alfred • Allegheny • American • Antioch • Babson • Bard • Barnard • Bates • Beloit • Bennington • Boston University • Bowdoin • Brandeis • Bryn Mawr • Bucknell
Carleton • Case Western Reserve • Centenary College • Centre • Claremont McKenna • Clark University • Coe • Colby • Colby-Sawyer • Colgate • Colorado College
Connecticut College • Cornell College • Denison • University of Denver • DePauw • Dickinson • Drew • Duke • Earlham • Eckerd • Elizabethtown • Elmira • Emory
Fairfield • Fisk • Fordham • Franklin & Marshall • George Washington • Gettysburg • Goucher • Grinnell • Guilford • Gustavus Adolphus • Hamilton • Hampden-Sydney
Hampshire • Hartwick • Harvard-Radcliffe   Haverford • Hobart & William Smith • Hofstra
Hollins • Hood • Johns Hopkins • Kalamazoo   Kenyon • Knox • Lafayette • Lake Forest • Lawrence
Lehigh • Lewis & Clark • Linfield • Macalester   **COMMON APPLICATION**   Manhattan • Manhattanville • University of Miami
Mills • Millsaps • Morehouse • Mount Holyoke   Muhlenberg • New York University • Oberlin
Occidental • Ohio Wesleyan • Pitzer • Pomona   University of Puget Sound • Randolph-Macon
Randolph Macon Woman's • University of Redlands   Reed College • Rensselaer Polytechnic • Rhodes
Rice • University of Richmond • Ripon • Rochester Institute of Technology • University of Rochester • Rollins • St. Lawrence • St. Olaf • Salem • Sarah Lawrence
Scripps • Simmons • Skidmore • Smith • University of the South • Southern Methodist • Southwestern • Spelman • Stetson • Susquehanna • Swarthmore
Texas Christian • Trinity College • Trinity University • Tulane • Tulsa • Union • Ursinus • Valparaiso • Vanderbilt • Vassar • Wake Forest • Washington College
Washington & Lee • Wells • Wellesley • Wesleyan • Western Maryland • Wheaton • Whitman • Whittier • Widener • Willamette • Williams • Wooster • Worcester Polytechnic

THE 1994–95 COMMON APPLICATION

WHY A COMMON APPLICATION?

The colleges and universities listed above have worked together to develop and distribute the Common Application. Many of the colleges use the Common Application exclusively. *Members encourage its use and all give equal consideration to the Common Application and the college's own form.*

Extensive experience with this form over a period of several years has demonstrated its advantages to both students and counselors. The "Application for Undergraduate Admission" must be completed only once; photocopies may then be sent to any number of participating colleges. The same is true of the "School Report" and "Teacher Evaluation" portions. This procedure simplifies the college application process by saving time and eliminating unnecessary duplication of effort.

APPLICANTS:

Steps for completion of Common Application:

1. Please fill out the application for undergraduate admission that accompanies this instruction sheet.

2. Have it photocopied for each listed college to which you are applying.

3. Mail it, along with the appropriate fee, to the office of admissions of each of the colleges you have chosen. Application fees and deadlines for each participating college are listed.

4. *If you are applying to one of the colleges as an Early Action or Early Decision Candidate, check with that college for their policy and deadline, and notify the college of your intent by attaching a letter to your application. You must also inform your counselor.*

5. Check in the box to the left of each college to which you are applying and give the sheet(s), along with the School Report, to your guidance counselor. He or she needs this list in order to send school reports for you to the colleges. Your school may charge a small fee to cover photocopying, processing, and/or postage.

6. If any of the colleges to which you are applying requests a Teacher Evaluation, ask a teacher(s) to complete that form as instructed and to mail a copy to the appropriate college(s).

7. A few of the colleges want additional writing samples. If you are applying to one of those, you may photocopy a paper which was submitted as a regular school assignment. The photocopy(ies) should contain the teacher comments and grade. You may also submit additional material, such as tapes of musical performances, photographs of art work, reports of scientific projects, etc.

8. Upon receipt of your application some colleges will request supplementary material. Complete this material according to their instructions and return as rapidly as possible. Some will give you a deadline date. Note this date is often different (usually later) than the application deadline.

9. Be sure that your counselor forwards to colleges to which you have applied transcripts covering your grades through the first trimester or semester of senior year.

10. *If you are using the Common Application computer disk, check specific college policy on accepting disk or printout. Each college's requirements are noted in italics at the end of its admissions information. Software versions available are Macintosh (MAC), and Windows and DOS for IBM-compatibles (IBM). Student options are (a) submit printout only; (b) submit disk only; (c) submit either printout or disk; or (d) printout required with disk.*

COUNSELORS:

When a student returns this form to you, complete a school report for him or her and photocopy the report for each of the colleges the student has checked. Then mail to each of those colleges a copy of the school report with the Secondary School Record or a legible copy of the "Transcript" form used in your school. If available, please enclose copies of the School Profile and "Transcript" legend.

Printed and distributed on behalf of the participating colleges by the National Association of Secondary School Principals, 1904 Association Drive, Reston, Va. 22091

Albion • Alfred • Allegheny • American • Antioch • Babson • Bard • Barnard • Bates • Beloit • Bennington • Boston University • Bowdoin • Brandeis • Bryn Mawr • Bucknell
Carleton • Case Western Reserve • Centenary College • Centre • Claremont McKenna • Clark University • Coe • Colby • Colby-Sawyer • Colgate • Colorado College
Connecticut College • Cornell College • Denison • University of Denver • DePauw • Dickinson • Drew • Duke • Earlham • Eckerd • Elizabethtown • Elmira • Emory
Fairfield • Fisk • Fordham • Franklin & Marshall • George Washington • Gettysburg • Goucher • Grinnell • Guilford • Gustavus Adolphus • Hamilton • Hampden-Sydney
Hampshire • Hartwick • Harvard-Radcliffe   Haverford • Hobart & William Smith • Hofstra
Hollins • Hood • Johns Hopkins • Kalamazoo   Kenyon • Knox • Lafayette • Lake Forest • Lawrence
Lehigh • Lewis & Clark • Linfield • Macalester   **COMMON APPLICATION**   Manhattan • Manhattanville • University of Miami
Mills • Millsaps • Morehouse • Mount Holyoke   Muhlenberg • New York University • Oberlin
Occidental • Ohio Wesleyan • Pitzer • Pomona   University of Puget Sound • Randolph-Macon
Randolph Macon Woman's • University of Redlands   Reed College • Rensselaer Polytechnic • Rhodes
Rice • University of Richmond • Ripon • Rochester Institute of Technology • University of Rochester • Rollins • St. Lawrence • St. Olaf • Salem • Sarah Lawrence
Scripps • Simmons • Skidmore • Smith • University of the South • Southern Methodist • Southwestern • Spelman • Stetson • Susquehanna • Swarthmore
Texas Christian • Trinity College • Trinity University • Tulane • Tulsa • Union • Ursinus • Valparaiso • Vanderbilt • Vassar • Wake Forest • Washington College
Washington & Lee • Wells • Wellesley • Wesleyan • Western Maryland • Wheaton • Whitman • Whittier • Widener • Willamette • Williams • Wooster • Worcester Polytechnic

APPLICATION FOR UNDERGRADUATE ADMISSION

The colleges and universities listed above encourage the use of this application. No distinction will be made between it and the college's own form. The accompanying instructions tell you how to complete, copy, and file your application with any one or several of the colleges. Please type or print in black ink.

PERSONAL DATA

1 Legal name: Richards, Eugene Everett _____ Male _____
                  Last   *First*   *Middle (complete)*   *Jr., etc.*   *Sex*

2 Prefer to be called: Gene _____ (nickname) **3** Former last name(s) if any: _____

4 Are you applying as a [X] freshman or [ ] transfer student? **5** For the term beginning: Sept., 1996 _____

6 Permanent home address: 125 Brookdale Road _____
                                              Number and Street
Brookdale, Johnson County, Connecticut 06123 _____
     City or Town   *County*   *State*   *Zip*

If different from the above, please give your mailing address for all admission correspondence:

Mailing address: _____
                              Number and Street

_____ Use until: _____
     City or Town   *State*   *Zip*   *Date*

Telephone at mailing address: (203) / 136-4434 _____ Permanent home telephone: (203) / 136-4434 _____
                              Area Code   *Number*   *Area Code*   *Number*

Birthdate: 5/4/78 ____ Citizenship: [X] U.S. [ ] Permanent Resident U.S. [ ] Other _____ Visa type _____
          Month Day Year   *Country*

7 Possible area(s) of academic concentration/major: political science, history _____ or undecided [ ]

8 Special college or division if applicable: _____

9 Possible career or professional plans: law, business, government service _____ or undecided [ ]

10 Will you be a candidate for financial aid? [ ] Yes [X] No If yes, the appropriate form(s) was/will be filed on: _____

11
| The following items are optional: Social Security number, if any: [1] [2] [3] - [4] [5] - [6] [7] [8] [9] |
Place of birth: New York, N.Y., U.S.A. _____ Marital status: single _____
                City   *State*   *Country*

First language, if other than English: _____ Language spoken at home: _____

How would you describe yourself? Check any that apply.

[ ] American Indian, Alaskan Native (tribal affiliation _____)   [ ] Mexican American, Mexican

[ ] Native Hawaiian, Pacific Islander   [ ] African American, Black

[ ] Asian American, Asian (including Indian subcontinent) (country ____) [X] White, Anglo, Caucasian

[ ] Hispanic, Latino (including Puerto Rican) (country ____)   [ ] Other (Specify _____)

12 **EDUCATIONAL DATA**

School you attend now Brookdale Country Day School _____ Date of entry Sept., 1992 _____

Address 256 Brookdale Road, Brookdale CT 06124 _____ ACT/CEEB code number 123456 _____
         City   *State*   *Zip Code*

Date of secondary graduation June, 1996 _____ Is your school public? _____ private? X _____ parochial? _____

College counselor: Name: Mr. Timothy Dwight _____ Position: College Advisor _____

School telelephone: (203) / 456-7000 _____ School FAX: (203) / 456-7002 _____
                    Area Code   *Number*   *Area Code*   *Number*   **APP**

⑬ List all other secondary schools, including summer schools and programs you have attended beginning with ninth grade.

Name of School	Location (City, State, Zip)	Dates Attended
none		

⑭ List all colleges at which you have taken courses for credit and list names of courses on a separate sheet. Please have a transcript sent from each institution as soon as possible.

Name of College	Location (City, State, Zip)	Degree Candidate?	Dates Attended
none			

⑮ If not currently attending school, please check here: ☐ Describe in detail, on a separate sheet, your activities since last enrolled.

⑯ **TEST INFORMATION.** Be sure to note the tests required for each institution to which you are applying. The official scores from the appropriate testing agency must be submitted to each institution as soon as possible. Please list your test plans below.

	SAT I (or SAT)		SAT II: Subject Tests (or Achievement Tests)			American College Test (ACT)	Test of English as a Foreign Language (TOEFL)
Dates taken/	5/6/95		6/3/95	6/3/95	6/3/95		
to be taken	10/7/95						
Scores	1,325/	?	Amer. His.	Eu. Hist.	French		
	Verbal	*Math*	725	750	675	*(Composite)*	

⑰ **FAMILY**

Mother's full name: Beatrice Raphael Richards   Is she living? yes

Home address if different from yours: _____

Occupation: Homemaker
(Describe briefly)   *(Name of business or organization)*

Name of college (if any): Hunter College   Degree: B.A.   Year: 1976

Name of professional or graduate school (if any): _____ Degree: _____ Year: _____

Father's full name: Lester Jonas Richards, M.D.   Is he living? yes

Home address if different from yours: _____

Occupation: Physician - vascular surgeon   (self-employed)
(Describe briefly)   *(Name of business or organization)*

Name of college (if any): Yale University   Degree: B.S.   Year: 1972

Name of professional or graduate school (if any): Coll. of Physicians & Surgeons Degree: M.D.   Year: 1976

If not with both parents, with whom do you make your permanent home: _____

Please check if parents are ☐ separated ☐ divorced ☐ other _____

Please give names and ages of your brothers or sisters. If they have attended college, give the names of the institutions attended, degrees, and approximate dates:

Roger Harold Richards, 23, Columbia University, B.A., 1994

18 ACADEMIC HONORS

Briefly describe any scholastic distinctions or honors you have won beginning with ninth grade:

Honor Roll, 9th 10th grades

High Honors, 11th grade

History Prize (top scholar), 11th grade

19 EXTRACURRICULAR, PERSONAL, AND VOLUNTEER ACTIVITIES

Please list your principal extracurricular, community, and family activities and hobbies in the order of their interest to you. Include specific events and/or major accomplishments such as musical instrument played, varsity letters earned, etc. Please (✓) in the right column those activities you hope to pursue in college.

Activity	Grade level or post-secondary (p.s.) 9 10 11 12 PS	Approximate time spent Hours per week	Weeks per year	Positions held, honors won, or letters earned	Do you plan to participate in college?
Travel: U.S., Europe	x x x x		6-10		
Tennis, JV, Varsity	x x x x	10-20	10	Letter (3 yrs) State champion, '94, '95	yes
Downhill skiing	x x x x	8-30	14	18 gold, silver, bronze medals, US, Euro comps	yes
Outside reading	x x x x	12	40-50		yes
Oil painting	x x x x	varies	40-50		yes
Tutoring children, Harlem Settlement Hse.	x x	4	30		?
Amnesty International	x	3	30		?

20 WORK EXPERIENCE

List any job (including summer employment) you have held during the past three years.

Specific nature of work	Employer	Approximate dates of employment	Approximate no. of hours spent per week
Clerk, office boy, "gofer" New York City law firm	Frank & Frank	6/15-8/30-1995	40
Janitor's assistant	Carr Publishing Co.	6/15-8/30-1994	40-50
Farmhand	Aaron & Joshua's Farm	6/15-9/6-1993	40

In the space provided below, briefly discuss which of these activities (extracurricular and personal activities or work experience) has had the most meaning for you, and why.

As explained in my personal statement on the next page, my summer work has had the most

meaning for me. Apart from that, my travels abroad and competition in European

ski championships have given me the chance to meet and become friends with many young

people from other countries and helped me learn more about and better understand

the history and culture of those lands.

When I was 14, I decided not to return to summer camp for a seventh year. Instead, I found my first summer job -- as a farmhand. Forty hours a week of planting, weeding, hoeing, cultivating and harvesting in the hot sun proved a back-breaking contrast to water-skiing, sailing, swimming and playing in the cool mountain area where I had gone to camp. But I quickly learned how difficult hard labor can be and to respect those who do it to earn a living.

The farm where I worked was a small one -- one of the two last in the suburbs where I live, near New York City. It also offers a lot of kids like me summer jobs to earn extra money. But unlike another farm I visited that summer, none of us kids needed the money we earned to survive.

Before the tomatoes ripened at the farm where I worked, the farmer would drive his truck a hundred miles to the south to the big commercial farms where tomatoes ripened earlier, and he could buy them for his own roadside stand. It was on a trip to buy tomatoes that I first saw migrant workers and their shacks, with no windows, running water or electricity. All the shacks were carefully hidden from travelers along nearby highways.

I had heard of migrant workers, but never realized how bad their lives really were until an 11-year-old Puerto Rican boy was sent to help us load our truck. He looked as if he hadn't washed or changed his clothes in days. He was caked with dirt. His jeans were worn, patched, torn and tattered. He touched my jeans to see what cloth on new pants felt like. He could barely hold his half of the 30-pound bushel baskets we lifted onto the truck. He told me he worked from 5 a.m. to 9 p.m. and earned 40 cents for each bushel he picked and loaded. He said he picked about three bushels an hour -- about $1.20 worth, or less than one-third the legal minimum wage for adults. He said he went to school "sometimes" when his family was down South in winter, harvesting in Florida.

I later learned that there are nearly 400,000 children under 15 like him, working illegally on thousands of American farms with their migrant-worker parents for illegally low pay and illegally long hours.

I have had several different summer jobs since then, including one last summer as a clerk in a magnificent Park Avenue law firm in New York City -- an opportunity that inspired me to think seriously about law as a possible career. But I will never forget that boy, an American like me, but one who seemed condemned to a life of poverty, illiteracy and near-serfdom as a migrant worker, with none of the hopes of young people such as I, whose opportunities are limited only by their own ambitions. I hope I can use my education to eradicate the terrible evil I saw that summer evening, when I first began working.

Albion • Alfred • Allegheny • American • Antioch • Babson • Bard • Barnard • Bates • Beloit • Bennington • Boston University • Bowdoin • Brandeis • Bryn Mawr • Bucknell
Carleton • Case Western Reserve • Centenary College • Centre • Claremont McKenna • Clark University • Coe • Colby • Colby-Sawyer • Colgate • Colorado College
Connecticut College • Cornell College • Denison • University of Denver • DePauw • Dickinson • Drew • Duke • Earlham • Eckerd • Elizabethtown • Elmira • Emory
Fairfield • Fisk • Fordham • Franklin & Marshall • George Washington • Gettysburg • Goucher • Grinnell • Guilford • Gustavus Adolphus • Hamilton • Hampden-Sydney
Hampshire • Hartwick • Harvard-Radcliffe   Haverford • Hobart & William Smith • Hofstra
Hollins • Hood • Johns Hopkins • Kalamazoo   Kenyon • Knox • Lafayette • Lake Forest • Lawrence
Lehigh • Lewis & Clark • Linfield • Macalester   **TEACHER EVALUATION**   Manhattan • Manhattanville • University of Miami
Mills • Millsaps • Morehouse • Mount Holyoke   Muhlenberg • New York University • Oberlin
Occidental • Ohio Wesleyan • Pitzer • Pomona   University of Puget Sound • Randolph-Macon
Randolph Macon Woman's • University of Redlands   Reed College • Rensselaer Polytechnic • Rhodes
Rice • University of Richmond • Ripon • Rochester Institute of Technology • University of Rochester • Rollins • St. Lawrence • St. Olaf • Salem • Sarah Lawrence
Scripps • Simmons • Skidmore • Smith • University of the South • Southern Methodist • Southwestern • Spelman • Stetson • Susquehanna • Swarthmore
Texas Christian • Trinity College • Trinity University • Tulane • Tulsa • Union • Ursinus • Valparaiso • Vanderbilt • Vassar • Wake Forest • Washington College
Washington & Lee • Wells • Wellesley • Wesleyan • Western Maryland • Wheaton • Whitman • Whittier • Widener • Willamette • Williams • Wooster • Worcester Polytechnic

The colleges and universities listed above encourage the use of this form. No distinction will be made between it and the college's own form. The accompanying instructions tell you how to complete, copy, and file your application with any one or several of the colleges. Please type or print in black ink.

STUDENT:
Fill in the information below and give this form and a stamped envelope, addressed to each college to which you are applying that requests a Teacher Evaluation, to a teacher who has taught you an academic subject.

Student name: ___Richards, Eugene Everett___
                         Last   *First*   *Middle (complete)*

Address: ___125 Brookdale Road, Brookdale, CT 06123___

TEACHER:
The Common Application group of colleges finds candid evaluations helpful in choosing from among highly qualified candidates. We are primarily interested in whatever you think is important about the applicant's academic and personal qualifications for college. Please submit your references promptly. A photocopy of this reference form, or another reference you may have prepared on behalf of this student is acceptable. You are encouraged to keep the original of this form in your private files for use should the student need additional recommendations. We are grateful for your assistance.

CONFIDENTIALITY:
We value your comments highly and ask that you complete this form in the knowledge that it may be retained in the student's file should the applicant matriculate at a member college. In accordance with the Family Educational Rights and Privacy Act of 1974, matriculating students do have access to their permanent files which may include forms such as this one. Colleges do not provide access to admissions records to applicants, those students who are denied admission, or those students who decline an offer of admission. Again, your comments are important to us and we thank you for your cooperation. These colleges are committed to administer all educational policies and activities without discrimination on the basis of race, color, religion, national or ethnic origin, age, handicap, or sex. The admissions process at private undergraduate institutions is exempt from the federal regulation implementing Title IX of the Education Amendments of 1972.

Please detach along perforation

Please return a photocopy of this sheet to the appropriate admissions office(s) in the envelope(s) provided you by this student.

Teacher's Name (please print or type) _____ Position _____

Secondary School _____

School Address _____
                    Street   *City*   *State*   *Zip*

BACKGROUND INFORMATION

How long have you known this student and in what context? _____

What are the first words that come to your mind to describe this student? _____

_____

List the courses you have taught this student, noting for each the student's year in school (10th, 11th, 12th) and the level of course difficulty (AP, accelerated, honors, elective, etc.). _____

_____
                                                               (See reverse side) **TE**

EVALUATION

Please feel free to write whatever you think is important about the applicant, including a description of academic and personal characteristics. We are particularly interested in the candidate's intellectual purpose, motivation, relative maturity, integrity, independence, originality, initiative, leadership potential, capacity for growth, special talents, and enthusiasm. We welcome information that will help us to differentiate this student from others.

RATINGS

Compared to other college-bound students whom you have taught, check how you would rate this student in terms of academic skills and potential:

No basis		Below Average	Average	Good (above average)	Very Good (well above average)	Excellent (top 10%)	One of the top few encountered in my career
	Creative, original thought						
	Motivation						
	Independence, initiative						
	Intellectual ability						
	Academic achievement						
	Written expression of ideas						
	Effective class discussion						
	Disciplined work habits						
	Potential for growth						
	SUMMARY EVALUATION						

Signature _____ Date _____

Albion • Alfred • Allegheny • American • Antioch • Babson • Bard • Barnard • Bates • Beloit • Bennington • Boston University • Bowdoin • Brandeis • Bryn Mawr • Bucknell
Carleton • Case Western Reserve • Centenary College • Centre • Claremont McKenna • Clark University • Coe • Colby • Colby-Sawyer • Colgate • Colorado College
Connecticut College • Cornell College • Denison • University of Denver • DePauw • Dickinson • Drew • Duke • Earlham • Eckerd • Elizabethtown • Elmira • Emory
Fairfield • Fisk • Fordham • Franklin & Marshall • George Washington • Gettysburg • Goucher • Grinnell • Guilford • Gustavus Adolphus • Hamilton • Hampden-Sydney
Hampshire • Hartwick • Harvard-Radcliffe
Hollins • Hood • Johns Hopkins • Kalamazoo
Lehigh • Lewis & Clark • Linfield • Macalester
Mills • Millsaps • Morehouse • Mount Holyoke
Occidental • Ohio Wesleyan • Pitzer • Pomona
Randolph Macon Woman's • University of Redlands

SCHOOL REPORT

Haverford • Hobart & William Smith • Hofstra
Kenyon • Knox • Lafayette • Lake Forest • Lawrence
Manhattan • Manhattanville • University of Miami
Muhlenberg • New York University • Oberlin
University of Puget Sound • Randolph-Macon
Reed College • Rensselaer Polytechnic • Rhodes

Rice • University of Richmond • Ripon • Rochester Institute of Technology • University of Rochester • Rollins • St. Lawrence • St. Olaf • Salem • Sarah Lawrence
Scripps • Simmons • Skidmore • Smith • University of the South • Southern Methodist • Southwestern • Spelman • Stetson • Susquehanna • Swarthmore
Texas Christian • Trinity College • Trinity University • Tulane • Tulsa • Union • Ursinus • Valparaiso • Vanderbilt • Vassar • Wake Forest • Washington College
Washington & Lee • Wells • Wellesley • Wesleyan • Western Maryland • Wheaton • Whitman • Whittier • Widener • Willamette • Williams • Wooster • Worcester Polytechnic

SECONDARY SCHOOL COUNSELOR EVALUATION

The colleges and universities listed above encourage the use of this form. No distinction will be made between it and the college's own form. The accompanying instructions tell you how to complete, copy, and file your application with any one or several of the colleges. Please type or print in black ink.

TO THE APPLICANT:

After filling in the information below, give this form to your college counselor.

Student name: ___Richards, Eugene Everett___

             Last   *First*   *Middle (complete)*   *Jr. etc.*

Address: ___125 Brookdale Road, Brookdale, CT 06123___

          Street   *City*   *State*   *Zip*

Social Security No. (optional) ___123-45-6789___

Current Year Courses—Please indicate title, level, and term of all courses you are taking this year: English (honors),
Math (Level 1), Amer. History, French 4, Biology (AP) - all senior, 1st Term

TO THE SECONDARY SCHOOL COLLEGE COUNSELOR:

After filling in the blanks below, use both sides of this form to describe the applicant.

This candidate ranks _____ in a class of _____ students and has a cumulative grade point average of _____ on a _____ scale.

The rank covers a period from _____ to _____. If a precise rank is not available, please indicate rank to the

                          (mo./yr.)   *(mo./yr.)*

nearest tenth from the top. The rank is weighted _____ unweighted _____. How many students share this rank _____

Of this candidate's graduating class, _____% plan to attend a four-year college.

In comparison to other college preparatory students *at our school*, the applicant's course selection is:

   ☐ most demanding   ☐ demanding   ☐ average   ☐ less than demanding.

How long have you known the applicant, and in what context? _____

What are the first words that come to your mind to describe the applicant? _____

_____

Counselor's name (please print or type): _____ _____

                                                                          Signature

Position: _____ School: _____

School address: _____ Date: _____

Office telelephone: _____/_____   Office FAX: _____/_____-_____

          Area Code   *Number*   *Area Code*   *Number*

School CEEB/ACT Code ☐ ☐ ☐ ☐ ☐ ☐

Please Note: Attach applicant's official transcript, including courses in progress. Include, if available, a school profile and transcript legend. (Please check transcript copies for readability.)

                                                      (See reverse side) **SR**

Please detach along perforation

Please feel free to write whatever you think is important about this student, including a description of academic and personal characteristics. We are particularly interested in the candidate's intellectual promise, motivation, relative maturity, integrity, independence, originality, initiative, leadership potential, capacity for growth, special talents, and enthusiasm. We welcome information that will help us to differentiate this student from others.

(Optional) I recommend this student: ☐ With reservation   ☐ Fairly strongly   ☐ Strongly   ☐ Enthusiastically

Signature: _____   Date: _____

CONFIDENTIALITY:

We value your comments highly and ask that you complete this form in the knowledge that it may be retained in the student's file should the applicant matriculate at a member college. In accordance with the Family Educational Rights and Privacy Act of 1974, matriculating students do have access to their permanent files which may include forms such as this one. Colleges do not provide access to admissions records to applicants, those students who are denied admission, or those students who decline an offer of admission. Again, your comments are important to us and we thank you for your cooperation. These colleges are committed to administer all educational policies and activities without discrimination on the basis of race, color, religion, national or ethnic origin, age, handicap, or sex. The admissions process at private undergraduate institutions is exempt from the federal regulation implementing Title IX of the Education Amendments of 1972.

cian in a high school rock group hurt his chances of admission by including a sound tape that began, "This is me playing with my rock group. We recorded it in my parents' garage, so there's a lot of noise from the street. But you'll get the idea." Not only did the admissions committee not get the idea, they were appalled by the applicant's poor standards of grammar as well as presentation. Artists and photographers should send copies of their portfolios, and gifted scholars (and even chess players) should send copies of any materials (e.g., newspaper clippings) that substantiate their exceptional talents. As in the interview, be modest and restrained in presenting your achievements. Don't be pompous. Let your achievements speak for themselves.

All colleges are eager to recruit gifted students, and some include with their applications optional cards for you to fill in about your talents in special areas such as science and math, the fine arts, and athletics. This helps the college identify talented applicants more easily.

20. *Work experience*: List only jobs held during the *last three years*. Again, use short answers.

21. *Personal statement*: The personal statement required on the last page is, of course, your essay. We'll discuss that a bit later in the chapter. Before that, however, I want to point out that the answers to most of the questions on the Common Application can be used in one form or another on other college applications. The questions may be phrased differently, but they call for the same answers. Some applications, for example, don't ask you to list your extracurricular and personal activities, but to describe them by answering what seems to be an essay question: "Which of your activities is or are more important to you and why? Please give us a relative indication of the time committed to each activity."

To answer that, simply take your list from the Common Application, and string the material together in sentences—for example:

> My most important activity is the editorship of the school newspaper. It provides me with an opportunity to talk with and get to know far more students and faculty members than I ordinarily would. It gives me a chance to see almost all the activities that make my school such an exciting community, and it gives me an opportunity to fine-tune my writing skills. I spend between two and three hours a day working on the newspaper, seven days a week.

Similarly, some schools may ask you to describe your work experience in essay form.

There are two other commonly asked essay questions. One is: "If you are interested in the arts (drama, dance, music and art), please give a brief résumé of your activities in this area. How do you plan to continue this interest in college?" The other question asks: "Name any office you have held in the student government or in other organizations and the year in which you served." Again, these questions merely ask you to extract items from your list on the Common Application and string together the details in complete sentences—such as: "I enjoy oil painting as a hobby and plan on studying art history and creative painting at college—strictly for my own personal enjoyment rather than for any career goals."

22. *Early action and early decision:* If you're a candidate for early action or early decision, you must attach to your Common Application a *neat*, typewritten letter to that effect. You may only apply early action or early decision (see page 118) to *one* college. So attach the letter to only one copy of the Common Application—not to all of them.

23. *Signature and date:* Finally, don't forget to sign and date the application before mailing it. The date, as I mentioned earlier, can be significant as an indication of your eagerness and your ability to organize your work. Last- minute applications are usually at a disadvantage (and may not even be considered if they arrive after the deadline). But aside from when you mail it, be certain your signature and the date are on every application, as required. In the case of the Common Application, sign it *after* making photocopies. Colleges do not accept copies of signatures. They must be original on each document.

Mail Early

The major reason for sending in as many applications as possible before the end of summer vacation is to get them out of the way. The first half of senior year is usually the hardest high school term academically and socially—and an improvement in your GPA during that term can often mean the difference between acceptance and rejection by the college of your choice. So, it's important that you be free to work your hardest and concentrate on academics.

In addition to enormous academic pressures, the first half of senior year produces a host of other pressures. Many senior athletes who were substitutes a year earlier are now first-string starters and team leaders; other seniors are now saddled with responsibilities to produce the yearbook or the school newspaper, or organize the prom. Still others are officers of the student body, with enormous responsibilities; and almost every senior has to fit in appointments for yearbook pictures.

If, in addition to these pressures, you also have to fill out incredibly long and complex college applications, and compose and write profound essays (or even miss some school days to travel for college interviews), you may find yourself with too little time to study or sleep, and probably no time to relax over Thanksgiving or Christmas vacations.

Although almost all your applications will arrive during the summer, printing problems may delay some until after you've started senior year. But if you've completely filled in practice copies of previous years' applications, you'll have nothing left to do but copy the material on the new applications. Use those older applications to get started as early in the summer as possible. If you have the actual application you'll be sending, make photocopies to fill in with pencil first as practice copies, so that you can continually erase answers and make other changes that will improve your application.

Learning to write a good application is a tough job, but you'll get better at it as the summer progresses and you keep rereading your original answers. Just like the interview, which we discussed earlier, filling out applications neatly and accurately is a skill that will serve you well throughout your working life. Now is as good a time as any—and indeed, an important time—to learn how to do it well, because doing a good job now with your college applications could well affect the future course of your life. Like any fine piece of writing, you should make many early drafts and constantly polish them until you have what you consider a perfect piece of work. Fill in all spaces in the practice applications—even your name and age. In that way, when you or someone else types the final copy for mailing, there won't be any questions about unfilled spaces.

As you fill in many of the applications, some of the efforts you made to display your enthusiasm about each college will now begin paying off. Many applications, for example, ask how you learned about the college: from guidance counselor, friends, visits to the college. "Two visits (including an overnight dorm stay) to the college" obviously shows the depth of your interest.

Often, the order in which various questions are asked indicates the weight they receive. Some colleges ask about your summer jobs first and extracurricular activities second—an indication they consider outside work important. Be certain you have beside you complete lists of extracurricular, athletic and personal activities throughout your high school years. List each item in order of importance. Be certain that your outside activities include intellectual and artistic as well as athletic and recreational pursuits. Top colleges are not terribly interested in applicants who find no spare time for independent reading outside school. Make sure you list any special awards you may have earned—not "Best Camper" when you were eight, but a ribbon you may have won in a recent horse show or for a painting you entered in an art show. In this area, too, early and careful preparation are important. A last-minute rush to fill out applications usually results in the omission of an important activity.

Except for essay questions, most applications are relatively simple to fill in and are self-explanatory. Some are terribly long, but they are simple if you organize your work carefully. If you have all your personal data in front of you in neatly organized lists, it will make completing your applications much easier. Filling in the Common Application first can be a big help here—even if you never use it. The applications are repetitive, so you won't have to be terribly inventive as you go from one to the other.

Again, use a pencil on practice forms to correct errors easily and simplify filling in final forms for mailing. Remember, though: There is *no excuse* for a misspelled word. You are applying for admission to college, and you are expected to know how to spell correctly! Misspellings will virtually destroy all the work you've done to this point. You're also expected to know more than just the basics of grammar and composition. No one expects you to be a professional writer, but you should be good at it if you expect to attend a competitive college or university. No matter what courses you take—yes, even science and math—you'll be writing a lot of papers requiring basic communication skills, skills in grammar and composition that permit others to understand what you write. Your sentence structure should be perfect. The meaning of each sentence should be clear, and the thought expressed in each sentence should flow logically into the next one. In short, you must be able to write properly and well. You must also be careful to answer each question as asked. There is no excuse for a college-bound student to list a class presidency, for example, under *academic honors*.

THE ESSAY

The essay questions are difficult—and for good reason. Once again, each college seeks to use a common measuring device for comparing applicants. An essay gives each student equal time and opportunity to display writing skills, originality, ability to organize material, emotional and intellectual depth, and maturity. The essay can also reveal a good deal about your personality—whether you're modest or conceited, concerned for others or selfish. As was the case in the personal interview, the essay represents one of the elements in the application process that is completely under *your* control, and it gives you an opportunity to display qualities not yet evident in the dry statistics and facts listed in the rest of your application and your high school transcript.

Application essays vary from college to college. Most ask for one basic "personal essay," in which they ask you to "tell us about yourself" or "tell us something about yourself you think we should know." The Common Application calls its essay a "personal statement," which will help admissions committees "become acquainted with you in ways different from courses, grades, test scores, and other objective data. *It enables you to demonstrate your ability to organize thoughts and express yourself.*" The italics are theirs, not mine, and they are used to emphasize the purpose of almost all college essays. Take those words extremely seriously.

As in many applications (though not all), the Common Application allows you to attach extra pages *of the same size* if your essay is too long for the space they provide. In contrast, other colleges insist that you write what you've got to say in the space provided; or they tell you to limit your essay to 200 to 500 words, thus testing your ability to write concisely and still make your point dramatically. In such applications, do not exceed the space allotted. Space limitations also test your ability to follow directions, which, in turn, is a test of maturity.

The Common Application gives you a choice of three topics, the most personal being to "evaluate a significant experience or achievement that has special meaning to you." A second choice is to "discuss some issue of personal, local, or national concern and its importance to you," and the third choice is to select "a person who has had a significant influence on you, and describe that influence." Other applications ask for a personal essay in broader terms, such as: "Write on a subject of your choosing," or: "We are interested in anything of importance to you that will help us better understand you: your abilities, your interests, your background, your aspirations." Whatever the essay question, it's the same for every applicant, and it gives each student an equal chance to show the kind of work he or she is capable of doing.

The personal essay is tremendously important. There's simply no way to overemphasize its importance—especially since so many colleges and universities have done away with personal interviews. That leaves the essay as one of the few ways the college has of getting to know you, the individual with unique characteristics that may not show up in the statistics of your school transcript and the rest of your application. The essay can, therefore, be decisive for many applicants at many colleges. I think it's impossible to find the time and energy to do a superior job on it during the crush of school activities in the fall of your senior year. So, by all means get it done in the summer before school starts.

Remember, you can probably use the same essay, word for word (or with only minor word changes), in every application. So, it should be a masterpiece—your masterpiece. It should, if possible, relate to those qualities discussed earlier that make you a unique individual. Depending on the way the essay is written, it may well be academically oriented, involving your differences with conventional criticism of a work of art, music or literature—or about a historical or current political event. "A subject of your own choosing" can range from a discussion of the Nuremberg Trials to the effects of seeing your first opera. It could be about a complex mathematical or physical theory, about science, about what it's like to be black in a white world (or vice versa). Don't pick mundane topics, such as "Delivering Newspapers for a Summer Job," unless you're a gifted writer who can turn the essay into a profoundly beautiful or exceptionally hilarious piece of prose.

The topic is often less important than the writing skills, originality, and the emotional and intellectual depth you bring to your essay. Remember that, whether you're aware of it or not, your writing, good or bad, will expose your personality. In one exceptionally original essay, a successful applicant wrote about himself from the perspective of others. Beginning his essay by asking, "What's John really like?" he answered his own question by inventing a series of often hilarious, short appraisals of himself by those who might know him best:

> ROOMMATE: The main thing about John is that he has good speakers. With his speakers and my receiver, we've got a really good system. But the guy is a slob! A disaster! He doesn't care about anything. The room is a zoo.
> FRIEND'S MOTHER: The kid is a real space cadet. All he does is lose things. This is the second time this month I've mailed him his wallet.
> HEADMASTER: Who? Oh, yes, a great kid, a great kid . . . . By the way, which John are you talking about?

The essay continues with other imaginary comments from girlfriends, John's mother and father, brother, sister, teachers, employer, coach, chaplain, etc., and ends with a comment from

> FISH IN THE FISH TANK: He cleans my tank, plugs in my oxygen and feeds me every day. I think John may be God.

Obviously, John is not only an exceptionally gifted and original writer, he's also modest enough to be able to laugh at himself and mature enough to recognize how others see him. Compare what I've showed you of his essay with excerpts from an essay by another applicant:

> As a human being, I am easy to get along with. I can make friends rather easily. I am a hard worker and strive to achieve my goals. I feel my best quality in life is that I set goals to plan in life. This gives me an outline in which to follow. The quality that I like least in myself is my sharp attitude. When someone asks me a question I jump at them, not meaning it. It's a habit in which I never lost. I am however easing up on it slowly . . . .

In addition to appalling grammar, sentence structure and lack of writing ability, the candidate has displayed so much conceit (count the "I's" and "me's") and concern with self that few selective colleges would consider such a candidate attractive. John's essay, in contrast, never even uses the pronouns "I" or "me." There are more sample essays in Appendix C. All were parts of applications to highly selective colleges. See if you can tell which candidates were accepted, rejected or wait-listed.

Most colleges tell you the reason they want you to write the essay is so that they can "become acquainted with you in ways different from courses, grades, test scores, and other objective data." Some essay questions may seem different, but are really asking the same thing in a different way. One application, for example, asks you to assume you've been accepted and your future roommate wants to know "what you're like as a person. Write a letter to your roommate introducing yourself in such a way that he or she can discover some of your strengths as well as your major character traits and goals." Like the Common Application, this application simply asks you to expose those elements of your own character that make you unique.

Now, not all application essays are the same. Indeed, some are quite complex. The essay requests of a recent Duke University application, for example, were not only different, they required a good deal of thought. Duke asked for two short essays, first, and then a longer one of no more than 500 words. The first short essay question asked, "Why do you consider Duke a good match for you? Is there something in particular you anticipate contributing to the Duke community?" That's a terribly important question that you really ought to think about carefully and consider answering for yourself for every college you apply to. Duke's second short essay question asks, "Consider the books you have read in the last year or two. Which is your favorite book or character and why?" Again, this requires a good deal of thought and a profound although short, answer.

The Duke application then gave applicants a choice of three longer essays, instead of the "personal statement" of many other applications:

"a. Please describe an experience that led you to question your values or change one of your strongly held opinions. How did you change as a result of this experience?

"b. John Keats said, 'Even a proverb is no proverb at all till your Life has illustrated it.' Please tell us about an experience in your own life which illustrates a proverb, maxim, or quote that has special meaning for you.

"c. Please write on a matter of importance to you. Any topic, and any form of written expression is acceptable. If you have written something for another purpose that you believe represents you particularly well, feel free to submit it here. As a guideline, remember that we are especially interested in issues of personal significance."

Not easy? Well, Duke like other highly selective colleges, is not looking for applicants who seek the "easy way out," or in the case of college applications, an easy way "in." They are looking for scholars, and the questions illustrated above are questions for young men and women with outstanding minds.

Your essay can add a great deal of weight to your application package. Write several essays if you can. Lay each aside, then reread them a week or two later. Remember, this may be the most important essay you've ever written. It is not a routine piece of homework you can dash off in a single evening or over a weekend while watching television. This is college-level work that will be carefully examined by college teachers and professors who can easily tell how much time you invested in it—and, by the way, if every word in it is your own, original work! (Whether you realize it or not, the original writing of a high school senior—no matter how gifted—is easily distinguishable from that of an older person.)

So give yourself as much time as possible. Start early in the summer and work on it regularly, rewriting, editing and polishing it, until you've put together a piece that will serve as a showcase of your skills, talents and special qualities, an essay that will prove that you deserve admission to the colleges to which you're applying. By all means show it to your parents and any teacher who can make suggestions for improvements. Every writer seeks constructive criticism, and you should too. In the end, however, it must be your own work.

Although some colleges ask you to write the essay in your own handwriting, most prefer it to be typed or printed by word processor. In any case, type the rest of the application so that it's legible. If you haven't learned to type or use a word processor yet, the summer of your junior year is as good a time as any to learn. Typing and word processing will help you in college, where you'll have too many papers to handle in longhand. Moreover, most college courses require that papers be typed.

Some applications ask for more than one essay—one about yourself, and an additional one aimed at displaying your intellectual and academic depth. One common essay topic asks you to select the man or woman, living or dead, you'd most like to interview if you were a journalist—and to tell why. For that kind of question, try to display some originality as well as academic depth. Don't pick someone everyone else will choose. An obvious choice such as George Washington ("because he was the father of our country") or Abraham Lincoln ("because he freed the slaves") could, unless brilliantly written, hurt the quality of your application. Again, Duke has used an interesting variation on this. "Today, young men and women no longer have heroes outside the home. Individuals who might have served as possible role models have been discovered to be too weak to emulate," says the application, which then asks, "Do you agree or disagree with this statement? Why? Please feel free to use examples." Trite, obvious, thoughtless examples will, again, lower the quality of your application. And don't, whatever you do, explain why some family member or teacher is "too weak for you to emulate." Always be positive!

Similarly, "My Summer Vacation" will— unless it displays exceptional writing talents, and emotional and literary depth— almost certainly cost you points in the consideration of your application, if that is your answer to the essay question asking you to detail an event that most influenced your life.

Another type of essay question that's sometimes asked in addition to the personal essay is: "Discuss nonacademic interests (extracurricular work or community activities) that have been most meaningful to you." Another college asks you to discuss briefly the one or two academic experiences (e.g., book, project or paper you have done; a specific course or subject you took in school) that has meant the most to you during your secondary school years. Still another college asks what independent research you might pursue if you have the opportunity as a college undergraduate; while another college asks you to "discuss more fully any academic/intellectual interests that are especially important or meaningful to you." Some schools may ask you to write a short essay describing what you "expect" to get out of college.

Some of the more difficult applications have four, five or more essay questions, in addition to the personal essay. One application asks you to list the books you've read in the past 12 months and the magazines and newspapers you read regularly, and to put an X by those required in school. Another asks you to list four or five books that made the most impact on you and to discuss one of them. One college gives you some space to use "if you wish to make any additional comments. For example, if there are any special academic problems that you feel have not been adequately addressed in this application."

Another application states that "a successful college community depends greatly on the intellectual and personal contributions of its individual members," and it asks you to "share with us what you believe other...students (at this college) could learn from you, both inside and outside the classroom."

I'm not going to pretend that's an easy question. It's not—and it's not meant to be. All of these are questions drawn from application forms of the most competitive colleges in the United States, which are seeking mature students of superior intellect. That last question is not something you can toss off in a couple of hours while watching television. You'll need days and weeks of concentrated effort and thought and introspection—and that's why I urge you to get started early if you're considering applying to one of the most competitive colleges.

Most college applications are far less complex, however, tending to follow the form of the Common Application. They only demand one personal essay, which, as I said before, you'll be able to use over and over again.

Your application must be NEAT. You will be judged on its neatness. If necessary, ask your parents or a friend to type out the application. If you can afford it, pay to have it typed by a professional. Be certain it is neat, accurate and complete. And be certain you answer the questions as asked! I cannot stress this enough. If the application asks you to describe "the *event* that most influenced your life," don't describe the *person* that most influenced your life.

EARLY DECISION

One other choice you'll face before sending in your application is whether or not to apply for early decision. You can apply to only one college for early decision. All applications to other colleges must then be for regular decisions. If you decide to apply for early decision, that college should be the one you most want to attend. Under early decision, you must submit your application early in your senior year—usually by October 1 or November 1—and the college you select promises to let you know early—usually before Christmas—whether or not it will accept you on the basis of the record you've achieved during your junior year. You, in turn, promise that if you're accepted you will enroll as a freshman at that college the following September, and that you'll immediately withdraw all applications to other colleges and universities— without waiting to see if you were accepted.

Make no mistake about early decision: It is a contract that you must fulfill. No, it's not a legal contract, but it's a moral one, and if you violate it you're risking personal disaster. One student applied to several colleges for early decision, was accepted by two, and withdrew one application. The college whose contract he violated immediately notified the other college, which then rejected the student and warned his high school of possible repercussions if they ever permitted another student to file more than one early-decision application.

In other words, the top colleges stay in touch with one another. If you violate a moral contract at one such school, it will let all the others know, and you'll probably be rejected by all. So, remember the word "character," which headed the list of the most important nonacademic factors top colleges consider in their admissions decisions.

It should be obvious that whether or not to apply for early decision is not a question to be taken lightly. There are many advantages and disadvantages, all of which must be weighed carefully and balanced against each other.

Early decision is of great benefit to colleges because of the enormous savings in processing and paperwork. Let's say a college accepts 70 percent of its applicants, of whom fewer than 40 percent (about 27 percent of the original applications) actually enroll. That means the school must go through the enormous costs of processing about four applications for every enrollment. When you're talking about a university that gets 10,000 or 20,000 applications, that's a lot of paperwork and a huge expense. By offering early decision to students it most wants to admit and who most want to go there, the college assures itself of a core group of superenthusiastic students in the next freshman class. If, say, it can fill one-third of the class with such students in December, the college cuts paperwork by one-third and can then be far more selective in choosing the remainder of the freshman class. It can afford to pick the strongest applicants from the remaining applications, because it has far fewer seats to fill.

What are the advantages for the student? Well, the most obvious is the avoidance of tensions that go with waiting to hear about college acceptances until spring, when colleges traditionally mail acceptances and rejections. Early decision in December allows you to enjoy a relatively relaxed senior year in high school while the rest of your classmates "sweat it out."

On the other hand, rejection of your application in early December can leave you in a deep psychological hole, knowing uncomfortably early that you've been rejected by your first choice of college. Remember, though, rejection of an early-decision application is not necessarily final at all colleges. Some simply defer such applications and reconsider them with the main pool of applicants in the spring. In case of deferral, only your feelings are hurt, not your final chances of admission.

As for your chances of gaining a favorable early decision, they are greater at some colleges than others, often depending on enrollment rates, which are available in college directories such as *Barron's*. The enrollment rate is the percentage of accepted students who actually enroll in the college. As a rule of thumb, if the enrollment rate is less than 50 percent—i.e., if less than half the accepted students actually enroll—your chances of early-decision acceptance are greater than they would be as a regular-decision applicant. That's because such a college is usually eager to increase the number of enthusiastic students who make the school their first choice and genuinely want to attend. By applying for early decision, you're sending the college a clear signal that it is your first choice; and, if you're qualified, that enthusiasm may improve your chances of admission. Again, read the viewbooks. Many colleges accept a higher rate of early-decision applicants than regular-decision candidates.

If a college's enrollment rate is greater than 50 percent, your chances of acceptance may improve by applying for regular decision, because the school's early-decision acceptances may well be monopolized by special-category students, such as the sons and daughters of alumni and big contributors, or by academic, artistic and athletic superstars. Many of these students have been actively recruited and urged in personal interviews to apply for early decision—an indication that their acceptances would be more or less routine.

Even if you are invited to apply for early decision—an indication the college wants you as a student and that you'll probably get in—it only makes sense to commit yourself to a college in December if you're absolutely certain that the school is indeed your top choice. If that's not the case, you may be better off waiting until spring. Chances are, if you're good enough to win acceptance to a college in December, you're probably good enough to win acceptance in the spring. By waiting until spring, you'll be able to pick and choose from among other colleges that have accepted you.

So, the answer to the early-decision question depends on (a) your enthusiasm about a specific college and (b) whether your chances of acceptance are really improved by applying for early decision. By all means apply for early decision to a college that indicates it wants you to do so, if that school is one of your top choices. As a rule, an early-decision application can do no harm, and it may dramatically improve your chances of admission at some colleges. (At a college that is indeed your top choice, you may well want to ask your interviewer whether applying for early decision would improve your chances of admission.) But don't apply for early decision to a college that is not near the top of your list, simply to avoid the pressures of waiting four more months. You may be sacrificing a chance to get into your reach college and, worse, you'll spend the rest of your life wondering if you might have got in by simply waiting a little longer. Wait the extra few months.

Remember, though: If you plan on applying for early decision, you must take your SAT I and SAT II tests by the end of your junior year so that the results are reported to the college by the October 1 or November 1 deadline for such applications. Without test results, your application will be incomplete and, therefore, invalid.

Rolling Early Decision

Many colleges also offer applicants an opportunity to apply for rolling early decision, on the basis of which a candidate may apply anytime during the normal application period (usually until mid-January or early February), and the college simply notes on his application that he is applying for early decision. Under this system, he is notified one month after he files his application, but is still under the same moral obligation to withdraw all other applications if accepted. The only difference between rolling early decision and conventional early decision is the filing deadline.

Early Action

Still another variation of early decision is called early action. Used by a few Ivy League colleges such as Harvard and Yale, early action differs from early decision in that it does not commit you in any way to attending any of these colleges if they accept you early. You file as early as you would for early decision, and you can apply to only one college. All your other applications must be for regular-admission notification the following spring. The early-action colleges agree, in turn, to notify you in mid-December whether you've been accepted, rejected or deferred, which, once again, means your application has been put back into the general application pool for reconsideration and notification in the spring. If you're accepted, you're under no obligation to attend. You can wait until spring when you hear from all the other colleges to which you've applied, and decide then.

RECOMMENDATION FORMS

In addition to the parts of the application form you must fill in yourself, you'll also find recommendation (Teacher Evaluation) forms for one or more of your teachers to fill in. You, however, must fill in the top portion of each form, typing in your name, address, teacher's name and position, high school and high school address (see page 103). Don't leave this for your teacher to do. In addition, supply your teacher with a self-addressed, *stamped* envelope in which to return each form to each college. And don't wait until the last minute to give them to your teachers. They will not be able to write thoughtful, effective recommendations if they're under deadline pressures and are swamped with similar requests from other students. As soon as your applications arrive in the mail, fill in the appropriate spaces of the Teacher Evaluation forms and give them to the appropriate people at school. Do it right away!

You'll also find a School Report form, to which your guidance counselor, college adviser or school principal will attach a school transcript with all your grades and school activities during your entire high school career. The report asks the school for an overall evaluation of you as a student and citizen of your school community. As with the Teacher Evaluation forms, you must fill in the top parts with your name, address and other information (see page 105). If you hand these forms in blank to your school office, no one will know to whom they belong. They'll be put aside. Your application will remain incomplete, and you won't even know about it. You could fail to gain admission to college because of carelessness with paperwork. So, assume your responsibility. Be careful, thorough and well-organized throughout the application process. Double-check everything. Use the checklist in Appendix B for help.

ORGANIZATION

As you now realize, the application process involves a lot of paperwork, but it's there and must be done, and it can only be done successfully through neatness and careful organization.

Before even beginning the application process, it's important that you set up an efficient filing system for all the forms, brochures, catalogs and correspondence. Lose or misplace a page from an application, send the wrong form to the wrong college, or make some other similar paperwork error, and you could throw away an opportunity to attend the college or university of your choice. It's one thing to be rejected because of low grades, but quite another to be rejected because of a paperwork error and in spite of high grades and a host of other achievements. To keep track of all the things you have to do, use the timetable and checklist in Appendixes A and B of this book. You may want to make larger copies of them and pin them on the wall above your desk.

To organize your paperwork, set up a filing system for the material you must keep. Buy a small filing box at a variety store or office supply store, or simply get a sturdy carton from the supermarket, but make sure the box is wide enough to hold 12-inch-wide manila filing folders. Then get some manila folders—two for each college to which you plan to apply. In one of these keep the correspondence and brochures of that college. In the second folder put all materials relating to the application and the application itself. Label the tab of each folder in pencil with the name of the college, followed by either "correspondence" or "application forms." Keep two or three special folders for SAT I, SAT II, ACT and AP test materials.

As you narrow down the list of colleges to which you will actually apply, pull out the folders of the colleges you've eliminated and set them aside in a safe place. *Don't throw them away.* You may change your mind later about applying. Make space on your shelf for thick brochures and catalogs, and simply put them in alphabetical order for easy retrieval. Don't clog up your filing system with unwanted and unneeded documents and brochures. As I mentioned before, you'll be flooded by unsolicited letters and brochures from many, many colleges, some of which you've never heard of. Recycle unwanted material immediately to avoid paperwork clutter that will reduce your efficiency.

Before handing in the recommendation forms to teachers, be certain you've "interviewed" them, as I suggested earlier, to determine whether they can see their way clear to giving you exceptionally good recommendations. Be certain they get to know you well. Tell them about yourself and your life at home and outside the classroom, so that they can paint a complete picture of you in their reports. It's important that they, too, know and write about some of your unique qualities that might not be evident in the classroom. Do the same thing with your guidance counselor or whoever will be writing the school report.

Make a calendar of deadlines, listing when each form must be mailed to each college. About three weeks before each deadline, politely check with each teacher and with the school office to see that all forms are indeed on their way or about to be sent to the appropriate colleges. Remember: It's your responsibility to follow up on every aspect of your application. (Your own application form, remember, should have been mailed before you even started the fall term, or shortly thereafter.)

If you're a candidate for early decision, all your forms, plus those of each teacher and the school, must be mailed early—usually to arrive at the college sometime between October 1 and December 1. Again, it's your responsibility to double-check that these forms are mailed out on time. Don't rely on others. Even the brightest teachers make mistakes and forget.

If it was not included with your original application, another form will arrive before or after Christmas vacation from the colleges you apply to. This form must be turned over to your high school office for them to fill in your grades for the first half of your senior year. Again, fill in your name and address at the top of the form and deliver it to the proper school authorities. Follow up at the end of the semester to see that it was forwarded to the colleges on time. Your application *will not be complete* unless the colleges receive this form. So, make certain that it is sent out.

SUMMARY

1. Self-evaluation—what makes you unique?

2. Correspondence with colleges
   a. Research the materials
   b. Reduce list of colleges and select those you want to visit

3. Campus visits—reduce list further

4. Personal interviews
   a. Rehearse carefully
   b. Check personal appearance, conduct, manners
   c. Reduce list to four to six colleges to which you will apply

5. Special interviews with coaches, professors, alumni

6. Filling in the application

7. The essays

8. Early decision
   a. Rolling early decision
   b. Early action

9. Recommendation forms to teachers; other forms to high school office

10. Organization—set up filing system for correspondence and applications

FINANCING | 5
YOUR COLLEGE
EDUCATION |

One of your biggest worries about college may be how you and your family will be able to pay the tens of thousands of dollars an education will cost at a highly competitive college. Well, please stop worrying!

Under no circumstances should you hesitate to apply to any of the most competitive colleges because you think they're too expensive and you can't afford it. The truth is you probably can afford it, no matter how high the tuition, room and board, and regardless of your family financial circumstances.

As I said before, the most expensive, competitive schools may actually cost far less than seemingly less costly noncompetitive schools, because they have more money for scholarships and student grants. Over the years, these prestigious, generally older, colleges have produced generations of wealthy alumni who have contributed billions of dollars to the endowment funds of their alma maters. Endowment funds are like bank accounts, generating millions of dollars a year in interest; and, depending on the wishes of each contributor, the interest can be spent for general purposes (maintenance, repairs, etc.), professors' salaries, research or scholarships to students who need financial aid.

In addition to wealthy alumni, the most competitive colleges generally have a larger proportion of wealthy students who put less demand on the available financial resources of their colleges. That leaves the students who need scholarships with a much larger reservoir of funds to tap. Almost half the students at Yale, for example, are from private schools and less than a half received (or needed) scholarships. That left Yale with a far richer pool of scholarships to distribute to students who do need financial aid.

Costs of attending Yale are now approaching $30,000 a year, and the *average* aid award to freshmen who needed financial help in the 1993–94 school year was $19,000, or more than 75% of the costs of attending. At Harvard, where annual costs are equally high, only about 45 percent of undergraduates need scholarships from the university, and Harvard is able to dispense more than $30 million a year to them. The average scholarship is more than $11,000, and the average total package (including loans and job) is more than $16,000. Scholarships at colleges such as Harvard can range from as little as $500 to more than $25,000, depending on need.

Financial aid is not, however, limited to the neediest families. The average family income of students receiving scholarships at Harvard was $54,000 in the 1993–94 school year. More than 1,000 families with incomes above $60,000 qualified for grants, as did more than 180 families with incomes above $100,000— and that's because colleges such as Harvard take into account *total* family needs in awarding scholarships. They know that even a family with more than $100,000 in annual income cannot afford the high costs of college if there are six kids at home to feed and educate and if special circumstances—a sick grandparent, for example—are draining family resources. Later on in the chapter, I'll show you all the factors that determine whether you qualify for a college scholarship or other financial aid—regardless of what your total family income may be.

FINANCIAL AID SOURCES

In addition to direct scholarship grants from the college or university you attend, a wide range of scholarships is available from other sources—some from the federal government, others from state governments, and still more from private organizations such as corporations, labor unions, fraternal organizations and foundations.

There are also many low-interest loan programs open to you as a college student and to your parents. Usually, if you can't borrow enough to complete your financial package, competitive colleges will lend you the extra funds themselves.

In addition to scholarships and low-interest loans, all competitive colleges reserve hundreds of on-campus jobs during the school year for students on financial aid. Student on-campus earnings from jobs provided by the colleges averaged $1,100 during a recent school year, and ranged from $500 to $1,500 depending on need.

We'll look at all these sources of aid later on. For now, though, it's important to keep in mind that all the most expensive, most competitive colleges will see to it that finances do not interfere *in any way* with your obtaining an education there. Many accept students on a need-blind basis. That means the admissions office doesn't know or care how much money you and your family have or earn. They're looking for the best students in the country—which is why the admissions process is so difficult. But once you're accepted, it means that you're among the best applicants for that college and the admissions committee believes that their college will be best for you. In other words, that college really wants you and will do everything to keep you, including helping you put together a financial package that will allow you to spend the next four years free of financial worries.

In contrast, a less expensive, less selective college with fewer financial resources might prove more costly if it cannot offer you enough financial aid to cover all your college costs.

So, look to the best possible colleges for yourself—and ignore costs. The costs will probably take care of themselves.

WHY THEY CHARGE SO MUCH

Perhaps you're wondering why competitive colleges don't lower their fees if they have so much money. Well, the fact is even students who pay the full $25,000 or more a year for attending such schools only cover about 50 percent to 60 percent of the college's actual annual costs of educating them. That's right: The actual cost of a year's undergraduate education at the most expensive private colleges is between $40,000 and $50,000—not the $25,000 they now charge.

The reason their costs are so high is that they have the largest libraries, the most modern classrooms and extensive laboratories, and the finest dining, living and recreational facilities of any American colleges and universities. They also have some of the most famous and highest-paid professors in the world: Nobel prize winners; renowned authors; famed composers, musicians, artists, poets, scientists, historians, economists, advisers to presidents . . . and so on. Scan the list of professors in the course catalogs of the most competitive colleges, and you'll see names known around the world. They command large salaries; and what colleges charge for studying with such scholars does not come close to covering actual costs. The difference, as I said before, is made up by earnings from endowment fund investments and annual contributions from loyal alumni. One day, you will be among them.

PUTTING TOGETHER YOUR FINANCIAL PACKAGE

Until now, we've only talked about your application package. But there's another package you'll have to put together before going to college. Regardless of your family's finances— even if your family can pay the entire cost of college and graduate school—you'll need to put together a financial package to keep costs at a minimum. Your financial package will consist of any or all of the following elements: your own and your family's contributions from earnings and savings; loans from private and public sources; scholarships from sources outside the college; government grants; and, finally, college scholarships.

The reason I said "finally, college scholarships," is to emphasize that your college will only give you a direct grant-in-aid (a scholarship) after you have exhausted all other sources of funds. That doesn't mean the college won't help you. What I said before is true: Every competitive school that accepts you will see to it that you have a financial package that will permit you to attend—and enjoy—your college years free of financial worries.

But before they give away their own funds, they have an obligation to see to it that you and your family contribute the most you can afford, and that you take advantage of every other available financial resource. Then they'll make up the difference to complete your financial package.

FINANCIAL AID APPLICATIONS

All students who need financial aid of any kind must fill out a form giving complete details of their own and their family's finances. The Free Application for Federal Student Aid (FAFSA) and other financial aid applications are usually available in guidance counselor offices or directly from the organizations and colleges that issue them. The colleges themselves tell you which forms to use—just as they tell you whether you should take the SATs or the ACTs.

Whichever form you use, you only have to fill it out once, indicating which colleges you plan to apply to by writing in the federal code for each college or filling in the college names and addresses. The Federal Central Processor will do the rest.

Some private colleges also have their own financial aid forms for you to fill out—in addition to the information you and your parents provided on FAFSA, the federal financial aid application. These forms may change from year to year, but in general, they want to know how much money you earned from all the jobs you held during the past year, and whether you have any assets, i.e., cash, checking or savings accounts, bank certificates of deposit, bonds or stocks. The forms ask how you obtained your assets and how much income they generate each year. The forms also ask whether you're the beneficiary of a trust, and whether you've been awarded any other scholarships. If you're a veteran, you'll have to list expected educational benefits from the military. If you're married, you'll need to give the same data about your spouse.

Next, you will have to provide complete financial data about your parents, and you'll have to give details about the rest of your family—how many brothers and sisters you have, how old they are, and many other things. In deciding how much aid to give you, the colleges need to know how many children your parents have to support. The colleges will usually give you more aid if your parents are also putting some of your brothers and sisters through college and show that they therefore have a greater need.

In addition to filling in one or more aid forms, both you and your parents will have to provide the college with complete, signed copies of your most recent federal income tax returns.

Filling in these forms and providing so much personal data may seem like an enormous task—and it is. It may seem like an invasion of your own and your family' privacy—which it also is. But remember: You're asking the college to make you a cash gift of thousands of dollars over the next four years for you to get an education that will yield undreamed-of opportunities the rest of your life. You owe the college a few personal details about your family and finances. In effect, it's asking nothing more than any bank asks on loan applications—and this is a gift, not a loan.

Deadlines

Just as you had to meet deadlines in filing your applications for admission, you'll also have to meet deadlines for sending in your financial aid applications. Miss a deadline, and you'll probably miss getting some financial aid. Again, be first in line. If you're last, there may be no aid left.

EVALUATING YOUR NEEDS

Once you've sent in your financial aid applications, the Federal Central Processor will use standard formulas to determine how much aid they think you need, based on aid given to students with similar needs in previous years. Your guidance

counselor has pamphlets showing you how to use their formulas to estimate how much aid they'll probably recommend that
colleges give you.

Regardless of the federal need analysis, all competitive colleges have their own formulas for determining aid to students.
That is why so many competitive schools also ask you to fill out
their own, more detailed financial aid forms.

In determining how much aid you'll need, the college financial aid office will put together an individualized budget based
on all costs that you'll incur during the school year. These
include all personal expenses, an allowance for travel home for
vacations, and everything else you can think of— and probably
some things you can't think of. No top college wants you to
sacrifice any of the joys of college life, such as football games,
concerts or parties, because you don't have the necessary funds.
The costs of all those activities are calculated in the budget they
put together for you.

But it's important to understand that, before giving you financial aid, every college will want to know—and has a right to
know—that you and your parents are contributing as much as
you possibly can toward your education. Based on the financial
aid forms you fill out, your financial needs are determined by the
difference between your expected family contribution and actual
college costs. That difference must then be covered by a combination of jobs, loans and scholarship grants.

Your parents are expected to contribute to your support during
your undergraduate years. The amount they must give is determined by their financial circumstances: how much money they
make, the value of their assets excluding their home, their annual
expenses, their age, the size of their family, number of children
attending college or graduate school, extraordinary medical bills,
and any other unusual expenses that might limit what they can
spend on your college education.

In general, parents earning up to $10,000 a year are not expected
to pay anything, while families earning $20,000 a year are ex-
pected to pay about $1,000. At $30,000 a year, the expected family
contribution at the average college goes up to about $1,500; to
$4,000 at $40,000; $6,000 at $50,000; $8,000 at $60,000; $8,500 at
$70,000; and $9,000 at $80,000. Those figures are for parents in good
health, at the peak of their earning power, with no unusual expenses, and only you to put through college. The expected contri-

butions drop sharply if, for example, they're putting more than one child through college or graduate school, or demonstrate other special needs.

The range of financial aid can be enormous for any family income group. It can range from several hundred dollars a year to more than $25,000. All aid packages are decided on a case-by-case basis. Here are examples of how Colgate University helped three different families during the 1994–95 school year. It cost $26,600 to attend Colgate that year: $19,510 for tuition, $2,690 for room, $2,875 for board, $145 for the student activity fee, and $1,380 for books, supplies, normal travel, clothing and incidentals.

Family:	FAMILY 1	FAMILY 2	FAMILY 3
	Single parent; two dependent children, one already incollege	Parents married; two dependent children, one already in college	Parents married; three dependent children, two already in college
Family income:	$19,244	$57,207	$102,116
Student's educational budget:	26,660	27,000	26,660
Family contribution:	1,325	10,525	11,675
Parents (from income and assets):	(225)	(8,900)	(10,575)
Student's (from summer work):	(1,100)	(1,625)	(1,100)
Financial need:	$25,275	$16,475	$14,925
Financial Aid:			
State Grant:	3,575		
Federal Pell Grant:	2,300	2,300	
Federal Perkins Loan:	1,500		
Federal Stafford Loan:		2,625	2,625
College Work/Study:	1,300	1,300	1,300
Colgate Scholarship:	16,600	12,500	11,000
Total Aid:	$25,275	$16,475	$14,925

As you can see from the above examples, even if your parents cannot afford to contribute anything to your college costs, you, the student, will be expected to make a contribution—and a sizable one at that if you have no one to support but yourself. Assuming you have no dependents, you will be expected to work full time in summer and part time during the school year, and to contribute a minimum of $2,000 to $2,500 a year from those earnings—$1,500 from your summer job and $1,000 from your on-campus job, which the college will get you.

If you have any assets—a bank account, certificates of deposit, stocks or bonds—you will have to contribute 35% of the value of those assets to pay for college each year. For some students that can be very painful—especially if they've been saving for years for a car or some other prized object. But no college will pay for your car, and you will be expected to spend 35% of those savings for your education. If, in addition, you receive veterans' benefits or other government assistance, you will be expected to spend the full amount of those funds.

In addition to direct contributions from earnings and assets, you will then be expected to tap every other source of funds available from government grants, outside scholarships and student loans before the college will consider giving you a scholarship.

GOVERNMENT GRANTS

The federal government awards eligible students outright grants for higher education. These so-called Federal Pell grants can vary from year to year, depending on the number of students who apply and the government budget for education. They're awarded on the basis of need, as determined from those same financial aid applications I mentioned earlier. In the 1994–95 school year, they reached a maximum of $2,300 a year. But it's difficult to determine in advance which students will be eligible for Federal Pell grants or how much each will receive. So, regardless of your level of need, apply—and apply early. You have nothing to lose and everything to gain. Failure to do so may make you ineligible for other aid. Before most colleges will give you a scholarship, you must apply for a Federal Pell grant first. It doesn't matter whether you get a Federal Pell grant or not, but colleges expect you to try before they'll give you any direct aid themselves. Schools and colleges have the forms.

FEDERAL SEOGs

For needier students, Federal Supplemental Educational Opportunity Grants (FSEOGs) usually up to $4,000 a year ($4,400 for study abroad), are also available from the federal government, which gives each college a fixed amount of funds each year to distribute to eligible students on a first-come, first-served basis. So, if you delay your application you may be shut out, even if your financial circumstances make you a logical candidate for such aid.

OTHER SOURCES OF DIRECT AID

Once you've obtained all available federal government grants, and have exhausted your own personal assets and sources of income, the college will expect you to apply for various outside scholarships. You can obtain complete listings from your guidance counselor or from one of the many catalogs on financial aid. Here are the most accessible sources:

1. National Merit Scholarship. The PSAT (see Appendix D) that high school juniors take in the fall is also a qualifying test for National Merit Scholarships, which are sponsored by the National Merit Scholarship Corporation and backed by a large group of more than 600 major American corporations, foundations and colleges. The scholarships are awarded on the basis of test scores *and* financial need, and range from $100 to $8,000 a year for four years, with actual awards determined by family financial circumstances.

2. State grants. Most states offer some form of aid to college students. Some of it is based on need, some on academic or other form of merit. Some carry provisos that the money be spent only at a college within that state, for example, or at a state-run college. Seven states (Connecticut, Maine, Massachusetts, New Hampshire, Pennsylvania, Rhode Island and Vermont) and the District of Columbia offer "portable"

scholarships for residents to use at out-of-state colleges. State grants can range up to $5,000 a year. In addition to universally available state grants, there are also many special state grants for disabled and disadvantaged students. Your guidance counselor should have all the pertinent information and forms to use to apply for aid from the appropriate agency in your state.

3. Local scholarships. Local organizations in many communities often offer college scholarships. Again, your guidance counselor should have a listing of these, and be able to tell you whether you're eligible and how to apply.

4. Corporation, trade association and labor union scholarships. Many corporations, trade associations and labor unions offer scholarships to members' sons and daughters. Have your parents check with the firms they work for, with the trade association to which those firms may belong, and—if your parents belong—with their labor unions. Check with each college financial aid office to find out what corporations, trade unions or other organizations sponsor specific scholarships for each particular college. Thus, Elizabethtown College, in Elizabethtown, Pa., for example, has received annual scholarships from Armstrong World Industries, Dial Corporation, Tyson Foods and United Parcel Service. All four companies operate major facilities in that area, and the scholarships they offer are part of an effort by firms across the United States to be good corporate neighbors by supporting education in their communities.

5. Fraternal organizations. If either of your parents belongs to a fraternal organization, club or volunteer group (Elks, Lions, Rotary, etc.), have them check to see whether their organizations award college scholarships to members' children—and how to apply.

6. Private organizations. Many private organizations and foundations based on religious or ethical beliefs, or on race or national origin also offer scholarships to students they deem worthy. There are, for example, scholarships available for Native Americans and Hispanics. The National Association for the Advancement of Colored People awards annual scholarships to needy African-American students. The National Achievement Scholarship Program uses PSAT scores to award special scholarships to top-scoring African-American students.

7. Reserve Officers Training Corps (ROTC). The U.S. Army, Navy, Air Force and Marine Corps will pay part or all of the cost of college plus $100/month allowance for qualified young men and women who want to earn a commission and a college degree at the same time. Students who apply must qualify physically as well as academically, and they'll spend some summers on active duty in the military. After graduation, they'll have to serve in the military for up to four years and remain in the reserves thereafter. The amount paid is determined by the amount of time the student is willing to serve after college, as agreed upon in the contract signed at enlistment. The nearly 1,000 colleges and universities that sponsor ROTC programs are listed in a special section in *Barron's*, and they include many of the most competitive schools in the country. If you have any interest in a career or even a few years in the military, ROTC programs offer a way to a free college education and an opportunity to serve your country.

8. College merit scholarships. Some colleges award so-called presidential, or merit, scholarships to students on the basis of exceptional academic achievements. These are awarded on merit alone, regardless of financial need, by each college president. However, they are more often available at somewhat less competitive colleges, in an effort to lure top scholars who might otherwise go to more competitive colleges. Although they may be as high as $10,000, they average $500 to $1,000.

9. Other sources. There are hundreds of other, less-known scholarships you might apply for. Many are listed in directories that should be available in your guidance office, school or public library, or nearby bookstore. You may want to glance through one of these directories. There are also many counseling firms that, for an often hefty fee, will help you apply for some of these relatively unknown grants. In the end, though, I think you'll find you've wasted a lot of time and money, because most of them are reserved for "insiders." Moreover, no counselor can guarantee you a scholarship—no matter how much money you pay him or her in advance. I strongly advise you to be very cautious in this area and to stick to the sources listed earlier in this section. Those eight sources and the colleges that accept you are the surest providers of scholarships—with no cost to you.

STUDENT LOANS

Once you've tapped every source of direct financial aid from government grants and outside scholarships, your college will expect you and your parents to borrow a reasonable amount of money from any of several low-interest educational loan programs. No college wants to saddle you with an enormous debt, but they will expect you to borrow at least about $10,000 over your college years to contribute to the cost of your education.

Federal Stafford Loans (GSLs)

The best-known student loan program is the Federal Stafford Loan, which allowed any dependent student attending school at least half-time in the 1994–95 school year, regardless of family income level, to borrow up to a maximum of more than $20,000 over the four college years. Except for upper-income families, interest on the loans is subsidized by the U.S. government—i.e., the government pays all interest on the loans while you're in college and graduate school and for six months after you complete your higher education. In other words, unless your family is at the highest income level, you pay no interest—and, indeed, *owe* no interest on the loans until six months after you stop attending school at least half-time or more.

Upper-income students can also obtain Federal Stafford Loans, but are responsible for paying interest on the loans while they're in college. These loans, in other words, are unsubsidized Federal Stafford Loans, but the interest rate nevertheless remains at the same low level (far below commercial loan rates) as subsidized Federal Stafford Loans.

Interest rates under the Federal Stafford Loan program vary from year to year and are set each June, according to the interest rates for three-month U.S. Treasury bills. Rates cannot, however, exceed 8.25 percent and have traditionally remained far lower. The rate for the 1993–94 school year, for example, was 6.22 percent; for the 1994–95 school year, it was 7.43 percent. In addition to interest, you will also have to pay a 3 percent "origination fee" and a 1 percent insurance premium when you obtain the loan, to cover processing and other costs. These fees are deducted from the amount you receive. Thus, if you borrow $1,000, the college will receive only $960.

Under the Federal Stafford Loan program, you can borrow the money from your local bank after the college notifies the bank of your acceptance in the college and enrollment therein. The bank then forwards the money directly to the college, and you won't have to begin repaying the principal until six months after you leave college or graduate school. In other words, you don't have to repay your Stafford Loan after college graduation *if* you enroll in graduate school within six months and continue your studies. After you've completed your higher education, however, you must begin repaying your loan, plus interest, according to a fixed, monthly payment schedule over 10 years. More flexible repayment plans may also be available, such as the extended repayment, graduated repayment and income-contingent repayment plans available from the direct government loans described below.

The total amount you can borrow while at college varies according to your grade level—a maximum $2,625 for dependent freshman, $3,500 for dependent sophomores, and $5,500 a year for dependent juniors and seniors. (You can borrow up to $8,500 a year as an independent graduate student.) Independent undergraduates and graduate and professional students (and, in special cases, some dependent students) may be eligible for additional, although unsubsidized, annual loans of $4,000 for each of the first two undergraduate years, $5,000 for each of the last two undergraduate years, up to the $23,000 Stafford Loan maximum. Such students can also borrow $10,000 a year for graduate school and professional studies.

The amount you can borrow each year as an undergraduate also varies according to whether you're an independent individual. The total amount of the Federal Stafford Loan debt you can accumulate as a dependent undergraduate is $23,000. As an independent undergraduate you can accumulate up to $46,000. To be declared an independent, however, you must meet one of the following qualifications: You must be at least 24 years or older; *or* married; *or* have legal dependents of your own other than a spouse; *or* be an orphan or ward of the court; *or* be a veteran of the armed forces; *or* be a graduate or professional student.

There's one other thing to remember about Federal Stafford Loans: Although the amounts you can borrow are tied to your family's income, they are loans to *you*—not to your parents—and you are and will remain personally responsible for repaying them. As you'll see later in this chapter, there are loans your parents can take out to help pay for your college education, but the Federal Stafford Loan is not one of them. It is *your* debt!

Direct Government Loans

By 1998, the largest percentage of student loans will be made by the government instead of banks. Applicants for these loans will apply through their college. A lot of colleges are already offering such loans, which merely removes your local bank as the middleman.

There are several options under the direct student loan program. The first is exactly the same as the Federal Stafford Loan described above—i.e., a loan that is repayable over the 10 years following the end of your higher education.

A second option extends the time of repayment, according to the amount you borrow during your college years. If you only borrow, say $10,000 over four years at college, you'd have to pay that back over 12 years. If you borrow $60,000, the payback time would be stretched to 30 years.

Still another option designed for low-income borrowers is a 25-year, graduated payback plan that will allow you to repay smaller amounts right after college, when your salary is low, and then increase the monthly payments as your salary increases in future years. Monthly payments range between 3 percent and 15 percent of your total income, which the Internal Revenue Service would report to the Department of Education. The remainder of the loan would be forgiven if it isn't repaid at the end of 25 years. The length of the loan can vary from 12 to 30 years.

When considering any of the extended repayment plans, however, remember that the longer the repayment period, the *more* you'll end up repaying. If, let us say, you borrow a total of $50,000 for your college education, you'd pay more than $650 a month over 10 years and only about $400 a month if you stretch the payment schedule out to 30 years, assuming an interest rate of 8.25 percent. But, the higher monthly payments over 10 years would total only $78,000 when you've paid off your loan ($50,000 in principal payments and less than $28,000 in interest payments), while the lower monthly payments of $400 over 30 years would total $144,000 when your loan is repaid—$50,000 in principal payments and a whopping $94,000 in interest, or nearly twice the total you actually borrowed.

Federal Perkins Loans

For needier students, the U.S. government subsidizes another student loan program called Federal Perkins Loans. These allow students to borrow up to $3,000 a year for undergraduate study (a maximum total of $15,000 for the undergraduate years) at 5 percent interest. Unlike Federal Stafford Loans, there is no origination fee or insurance premium, and repayment of principal and interest does not begin to accrue until nine months after completion of your higher education, but it must be repaid over a 10-year period. Like Federal Stafford Loans, Congress can change the amounts and interest any time. (Graduate students can borrow up to $5,000 a year and a total of $30,000 under the Federal Perkins Loan program.) Like the Federal Stafford Loan, too, a Federal Perkins Loan is a loan to *you*, and you remain responsible for repaying it, not your parents.

Loan Deferments and Cancellations

Under certain circumstances, you can obtain deferments and even cancellations of certain federal education loans. As mentioned above, repayment of your loans will be deferred if you enroll at least half-time in graduate school. In addition, you can obtain a deferment on both the Federal Perkins Loan and Federal Stafford Loan for up to three years after ending your higher education if you cannot find a full-time job or you can prove you're suffering economic hardship. Both loans are automatically canceled if you become permanently disabled or if you die.

You can also earn up to 100 percent cancellation of your Perkins (but not Stafford) Loan if you decide on any of the following types of full-time occupations after completing your higher education:

- Teacher in a designated elementary or secondary school serving students from low-income families.
- Special-education teacher—includes teaching disabled children in a public or other nonprofit elementary or secondary school.
- Qualified professional provider of early intervention services for the disabled.
- Teacher of math, science, foreign languages, bilingual education, or other subjects designated as teacher-shortage areas.
- Employee of a public or nonprofit child-service or family-service agency, providing services to high-risk children and their families from low-income communities.
- Nurse or medical technician.
- Law-enforcement or corrections officer.
- Staff member in a Head Start program.

You can earn forgiveness for up to 70 percent of your Perkins Loan for service as a Peace Corps or VISTA volunteer and up to 50 percent cancellation for service in the U.S. Armed Forces.

Foreign Students

To receive federal student aid, you must be a U.S. citizen, a U.S. national (American Samoan or other territorial native) or a U.S. permanent resident with an I-151, I-551 or I551C Alien Registration Receipt Card. There are several exceptions—e.g., if you've been granted refugee status or granted asylum by the U.S. Immigration and Naturalization Service.

Keeping Up to Date

In any given year, Congress can (and often does) change the amounts of money it earmarks for higher education grants and loans. It's important to keep up to date, and fortunately, the U.S. Department of Education makes that task amazingly simple. Each year, they publish a free, easy-to-follow booklet entitled *The Student Guide—Financial Aid from the U.S. Department of Education*. It is essential that you and your parents obtain a copy. If you can't get a copy from your guidance counselor, write to the Federal Student Aid Information Center, P.O. Box 84, Washington, D.C. 20044, or telephone 1-800-572-5580. And, remember that the booklet is *free*. Don't let some unscrupulous "college advisor service" try to sell it to you. Indeed, the Federal Student Aid Information Center at the Department of Education would like you to report the name and address of any organization that tries to charge you for the booklet.

COLLEGE SCHOLARSHIPS

Once you and your family have exhausted all sources of financial aid, if there is still a gap between the money you've raised and the costs of attending college, many competitive colleges will make up the difference with a scholarship or outright grant based on your financial needs—regardless of any other scholarships you may have received (including possibly a merit scholarship from the college itself).

I realize this may seem confusing, because most students (and their parents) have the idea that financial aid starts with a "college scholarship," i.e., a grant from the college. But that's not the way it works. A college scholarship is usually the last element in most financial aid packages—the "gap-closing" element that ensures your attending the college of your choice free of financial worries.

Like your application package, the financial aid package is made up of many details that make it seem more complex than it really is; but putting it together is really quite straightforward. All the details are listed, in order, in the summary at the end of this chapter. To review quickly, though: Your first step is to fill out financial aid applications from the multiple data entry services that automatically send such application forms to the colleges you've applied to and to government agencies that issue student grants. You may also have to fill out individual college financial aid forms that will be included with your admissions application. You'll have to include with these aid applications signed copies of your own and your parents' most recent federal income tax forms. Make copies of all these income tax forms for inclusion in any other scholarship applications you may make.

You'll then begin putting together your financial package. First, you and your parents will make contributions from your assets and annual earnings, according to what you can afford. Second, you'll apply for one or both of two federal government grants and any state grants that may be available in your area. Third, you'll apply for one or more need-based scholarships and any merit scholarships for which you may be eligible. Fourth, you'll apply for any student loans for which you're eligible, and *then* the college will award you a scholarship or grant to close any financial gap between actual costs of attending and the funds available to you from other sources.

If, for some reason, though, the college financial aid office offers you a grant that does not close that gap, you and your family should not hesitate to negotiate. Do not simply walk away believing you cannot afford to attend. As I said before, *no highly competitive college will keep you from attending because you cannot afford to do so.* If there are some extenuating financial circumstances that the aid office may have overlooked, make an appointment to discuss them. Don't, in other words, be afraid to negotiate or have your parents negotiate.

If, for example, your first-choice college offers you considerably less financial aid than your second- or third-choice school, call up the financial aid office and tell them! Colleges are very flexible when it comes to disbursing financial aid. Like ordinary people, they want to spend as little as possible! It's up to you and your family to squeeze the most you can out of them. Reporting on just this topic, the *New York Times* told of one student who was offered financial aid of $13,000 by Vanderbilt University, $8,300 by Northwestern University and a mere $2,140 by Duke University. Total annual costs of education at each of the three universities was about $25,000 at the time, and the student had made Duke his first choice. He called Duke's financial aid office and reported what the other two colleges had offered him, and the next day, Duke increased its financial aid offer to $14,250 a year, saying it had "erred in calculating" the original aid package.

Although Duke's financial aid director insisted his office does not bargain with students over financial aid, he said he was always willing to review aid packages—especially if there are any changes in the family's financial status.

And there is something else to remember: Even if you're not eligible for aid this year, don't hesitate to reapply at any time and as often as you want during your college years, if your financial circumstances change or your costs of attending rise so high that you think you're eligible. I promise you that your college will try to help you if it's one of the truly competitive ones.

WHAT IF YOU'RE NOT ELIGIBLE FOR FINANCIAL AID?

Needy students seldom have any problems getting financial aid, but many students from middle-income families do, and the costs of higher education can put severe financial strains on such families. There's no need to endure such strains, however, because there are many ways for every family in every income group to cut those costs substantially.

Even if your family income is too high to qualify for financial aid from government grants or college scholarships, you may still qualify for merit scholarships of the kind mentioned earlier. These scholarships are given on the basis of academic achievement—i.e., merit—rather than financial need. Many colleges offer them, as do many states, towns and private organizations. So be sure to ask the colleges that accept you, and check with your guidance counselor for information about any merit scholarships from your state or area. Even the National Merit Scholarship Corporation makes token merit awards, regardless of need.

Low-Cost Loans

In addition to applying for merit scholarships, there are many other strategies to reduce the high costs of college. For one thing, remember that the vast majority of students—*regardless of income level*—are eligible for low-cost Federal Stafford Loans discussed earlier. Even at the highest family income levels, you can obtain an *unsubsidized* Federal Stafford Loan, which simply means you or your family will have to pay the interest on the loan while you're in school. (The U.S. Government pays it for lower-income students obtaining subsidized Federal Stafford Loans.)

Even so, the Federal Stafford Loan represents a far lower-cost loan than a standard personal loan from a commercial bank and, therefore, considerable savings for you and your family. The only conceivable disadvantage of the Federal Stafford Loan is that the interest payments are not deductible from income taxes, but interest on personal loans are not deductible either.

In addition to low-cost federal education loans, check with your guidance counselor to see whether your state offers any state-backed, low-interest loans to college students.

Other Loan Plans

In addition to Federal Stafford Loans, which you, the student, are responsible for paying back, there are loan plans for your parents to use in helping you pay for your college education:

1. Federal PLUS Program. Like Federal Stafford Loans, Federal PLUS loans are guaranteed by the U.S. Government. PLUS loans differ, however, in that they are loans to your parents rather than to you, the student. They allow your parents to borrow much more than you can borrow. Indeed, they can borrow up to the total cost of your education, minus all other financial aid you may have received. They can only do so, however, if you are declared their dependent on their income tax forms. Interest rate is variable, but capped at 9 percent. There is also an origination fee of 3 percent and an insurance premium of 1 percent. All loan proceeds go directly to your school, and unlike federal student loans, repayment begins 60 days after the money is loaned. Repayment is spread over 10 years.

2. Other parent loan plans. Many colleges, in conjunction with private lending organizations, offer tuition payment plans that allow parents with incomes of $20,000 to $100,000 to borrow the total cost of your college education (less any money received in financial aid grants) at the same low interest rate as a Federal Stafford Loan. The program allows your parents to pay for your education in monthly installments at low rates, instead of paying huge lump sums at the beginning of each school term. Your parents have to fill out only one application for the four years. An extended repayment plan allows them to pay in smaller monthly installments over 10 years if they do not want to pay the loan back

in four years. The interest rate, however, can vary throughout the repayment period and is not tax deductible.

3. SHARE Loans. This is a loan plan sponsored by the Consortium on Financing Higher Education, of which many of the most highly competitive colleges are members. There are no income restrictions for SHARE loans, but they are subject to the same rigorous credit checks that any bank would demand. SHARE allows your parents to borrow up to $15,000 a year for your college costs at either a fixed or variable interest rate, which, again, is not tax deductible.

OTHER WAYS TO CUT COLLEGE COSTS

One is to take advantage of tuition prepayment plans that many colleges offer. These plans guarantee you against any future rises in the costs of attending if you pay for all four years in one lump sum at this year's rate, when you begin freshman year. At the rate college costs have increased over the last decade, that's like earning 10 percent to 12 percent on your money, tax free.

A second way to cut college costs is to take advantage of loans, such as home mortgages, whose interest is tax deductible. If your parents have paid all or most of the original mortgage on their house or apartment, they can obtain a new mortgage, borrowing only what they'll need for your college costs, and deduct all origination fees and interest costs. Interest on home equity loans, which are second mortgages, is also tax deductible.

Another method of financing college costs is to sell enough stock to cover those costs, then repurchase the same stock on margin (i.e., buy it back with a loan from the broker). If the stock is sold at a loss, your parents can deduct some of that loss from current income taxes. Moreover, they can then deduct the interest on the broker loan to repurchase the stock, because interest on broker loans *for investment purposes* is tax deductible. Were your parents simply to borrow money against the stock to pay for your college, the interest would not be deductible. So, on paper at least, the loan must be for the purpose of investing in stocks or other securities.

Using any of these borrowing methods in combination with a tuition prepayment plan would make such loans almost interest free.

SUMMARY

1. Applying for financial aid
   a. Fill out financial aid applications
   b. Fill out the college's own financial aid forms
   c. Send signed copies of your own and your parents' most recent federal income tax forms

2. Putting together a financial package
   a. Your contribution from assets and earnings
   b. Your parents' contributions from assets and earnings
   c. Federal government grants
      i) Federal Pell Grants
      ii) Federal SEOGs
   d. State grants (ask guidance counselor)
   e. Need-based scholarships
      i) National Merit Scholarships
      ii) Local scholarships through your high school
      iii) Corporation, trade association, labor union scholarships
      iv) Fraternal organizations
      v) Private organizations (foundations based on religious or ethical beliefs, race, national origin)
      vi) ROTC
   f. Merit scholarships (based on academic or athletic achievements)
   g. Obscure scholarships (listed in directories)
   h. Student loans
      i) Federal Stafford Loans
      ii) Federal Perkins Loans
      iii) Loans from your college
   i. Parent loans
      i) Federal PLUS loans
      ii) Tuition payment loans
      iii) SHARE loans

3. Other ways to cut costs
   a. Tuition prepayment plans
   b. Home mortgages
   c. Home equity loans
   d. Broker loans

A FINAL WORD | 6
(and A Note to Parents)

I hope you'll gain admission to the college of your choice and spend four happy years there—and there is no reason you won't if you follow *to the letter* the procedures outlined in this book. Remember, though, two of those procedures include getting high enough grades and filling your high school years with meaningful extracurricular and community activities. The quality of those activities, don't forget, is far more important than the quantity.

When you receive your acceptances and decide which college you want to attend, remember to send in your deposit at least two weeks before the deadline—and send it registered mail, return receipt requested. Be sure to notify the other colleges of your decision to enroll elsewhere.

Regardless of which college you attend, remember that the vast majority of American colleges and universities rank among the world's finest. At almost every college in the United States you'll find all the books you need to get the world's finest education. The education is there for the taking. In the end, it's up to you, not the college, to decide what kind of education you'll get during your four-year collegiate career.

If, for one reason or another, you don't win admission to the college you'd most like to attend, don't be discouraged. In the first place, colleges make many mistakes in their admissions decisions. That's inevitable with so many thousands of appli-

cants. Secondly, many colleges reject thousands of highly qualified students who could do very well there. Again, that's inevitable
given the huge number of applicants, most of whom have almost
identical qualifications. Indeed, many rejected applicants later
turn out to be superstars at other colleges and later in life.

WAIT-LISTING

It is perfectly possible, of course, that you may be wait-listed
by the college or university of your choice and accepted by one
or more safety schools. If you can afford it, by all means send a
deposit (nonrefundable) to the safety school you prefer and
then wait to see whether your first choice eventually finds a
place for you.

Each college accepts far more students than will eventually
enroll. It's a risk that each college is forced to take—like airlines
and hotels that overbook because they know that a lot of
travelers will be no-shows and leave unoccupied seats or
rooms. Similarly, in the college application business, every
college knows it is not the first choice of every applicant. So, the
college overaccepts, knowing that students who applied to it as
a safety school will not enroll if they're accepted by a college
higher up on their list of choices.

In many cases, the number of students who actually enroll
falls short of the number of available seats in the freshman
class—and the college invites (in order of preference) the students on its wait-list to enroll.

If you should win acceptance this way, you'll immediately
have to send them a deposit and you'll lose your deposit at your
safety school. In all fairness to students on the wait-list at your
safety school, have the courtesy to withdraw immediately and
allow the school to fill your seat with another student.

REJECTIONS

If your top college choice turns you down, and you're still
determined to gain admission, there are really only two ways
to proceed.

One is to contact the admissions office: Ask for an interview; ask whether they'll review your application once more; and ask whether repeating senior year and reapplying the following year would improve your chances of admission. In all likelihood, it will not; and this is not an approach that I would recommend, because of the psychological dangers of refusing to accept rejection. Rejection by a selective college rarely reflects a student's qualifications. The college application business is, as I showed you in Chapter 3, partially a numbers game in which many less-qualified students receive preferential treatment, thus leaving fewer seats for many more-qualified applicants. It's terribly disheartening for a highly qualified student to be turned down in favor of seemingly less-able applicants, but it's important to learn—and accept the fact—that, fairly or unfairly, one's life can be affected by forces outside one's control.

TRANSFER

A far healthier approach—and one more likely to succeed—is to go to one of the colleges that accepted you and produce the kind of college GPA and extracurricular record that would make you an attractive candidate for transfer at the end of your freshman or sophomore year. You may find, however, that your success may be so gratifying that you'll decide to stay the entire four years—especially if, as I urged earlier, you picked safety schools you truly liked and wanted to attend—schools that were as right for you as your reach schools.

The process of applying for transfer is much the same as that of applying for admission to college as a high school senior. The only major difference is that your grades and general level of achievement will have to be superior enough to prove that your current college is simply not enough of a challenge for you—that you need to "step up" to fulfill your academic goals. Another valid reason for transfer could be your current college's inability to provide the facilities or departmental strength to allow you to pursue studies in a specialized field that interests you.

You'll still have to have a superior academic record to be considered for transfer, however. To gauge your chances, check the college directories and the college viewbooks. They list the number of transfer openings available each year at most colleges. Again, remember that legatees and special applicants will still have preference. Remember, too, that it's rare for more than 10 percent to 20 percent of transfer applicants to gain admission to the most prestigious U.S. colleges, although the percentage varies widely from year to year. State universities have far more openings for transfer students than the most competitive private colleges. Quite simply, the number of openings depends on the number of students who flunk or drop out; and no more than two percent, and usually less than one percent, of the students leave the most prestigious schools such as Yale or Harvard. They struggled too hard to get in, and few are willing to relinquish their opportunities.

So don't look to transferring as an extremely viable method of gaining admission to your first choice of college, if it's one of the most competitive. The best method, and the one most likely to succeed, is to get to work now, while you're in high school, building an outstanding record—and outstanding application package—one so fine that the most selective colleges will gladly open their doors to you.

Even if you're a senior with a less-than-sparkling record during your first three years of high school, a superior effort during the first half of your senior year will at least get you into college. If you're still a junior—or better yet, a sophomore or freshman—you have plenty of time to make this your best year ever and to improve on that record next year. So begin now—with tonight's homework—to turn your high school career into one that will show every college the kind of person you really are and the kind of work you can do. You can do it. You can get into a top college—into the college you'd most like to attend.

And don't be afraid to get help. Getting into college is a complex and difficult challenge that you shouldn't have to face entirely on your own. Your guidance counselor and teachers can be of great help—and so can your parents. Read the next section, which I've written for your parents, and then have them read it, so they can learn how to give you the kind of help you can use.

But remember, in the end, your work at school is what will determine whether or not you get into the school of your choice. Start now—and good luck.

A NOTE TO PARENTS

This book is also designed for parents who want to help their sons and daughters through the exhausting process of applying to college. Getting into a challenging college or university can and should be a family as well as an individual triumph—just as birthdays, weddings, anniversaries and holidays are family celebrations. Parents who rely entirely on high school advisers to guide their children through the college application process are not only risking serious disappointments and errors, but are also shirking their responsibilities as parents. Even the most costly, prestigious, college-oriented prep school cannot and almost will not assure each student's admission into the most challenging colleges or universities. They tend to guide the students who rank highest in their class into the most prestigious colleges, and the rest into safer collegiate havens that may or may not be in the best long-term interests of those students.

COLLEGE ADMISSION PROCEDURES

What can parents do to help?

First, let me suggest what not to do. Try not to add to the emotional and psychological pressures your son or daughter is already experiencing at school by nagging and expressing your own anxieties about college admissions. Surprisingly, the worst pressures at college admissions time come from other students—not teachers, guidance counselors or colleges. That's because the college admissions process is usually the first major competition in life for most young people. Each day at school, other classmates—some friends, some enemies—almost continuously discuss college admissions, repeating false, nonsensical rumors about how high school officials prevented this student from getting into college—and helped that one get in. In short, each day at school plunges every high school senior and many juniors into a storm of truths, half-truths, falsehoods, rumors, expectations and fears about the complex admissions process. They don't need any more storms at home—and they don't need to hear any more half-truths and rumors from neighbors and family friends. What you hear from your adult friends and relatives about the college admissions process is usually utter nonsense. Regardless of how many of their children have gone to college, your friends and neighbors are probably not authorities on the college admissions process. So, for your children's sake, ignore what you hear from well-meaning friends, relatives, neighbors, golf and tennis partners, and business associates. Turn instead to reliable reference books and authorities at colleges for the information you need.

I hope this book will serve as a source of truths that will allow parents and students to approach college admissions calmly. I hope it will allow students to go to school each day assured they are on the proper road—regardless of the rumors they hear from classmates. And I hope it will allow parents to avoid the common error of adding to the pressures the college admissions process puts on their children. In Appendixes A and B there are a sample timetable and checklist of all the steps involved in the college admissions process; and there are handy summaries of information at the end of each chapter of this book. Many colleges also provide timetables and checklists for their particular application process. By following these efficiently, parents and students should together be able to handle the entire process easily, calmly and unemotionally—the way they'd handle any other major family event. There is no reason for panic. By all means be excited, but don't panic.

OTHER WAYS PARENTS CAN HELP

Aside from providing students with a calm, happy, pressure-free home atmosphere, there are other practical ways parents can contribute to the college application process. One obvious way is to learn as much about the process as possible—by reading this and other books, and by obtaining all necessary information on admission requirements.

Different colleges require different amounts of high school English, mathematics, history, science and modern languages. Check your child's curriculum at the beginning of each high school year to see that it fulfills the requirements of every college and university that might eventually interest him or her. Failure to meet those requirements may mean summer school or, worse, prevent your son or daughter from attending many desirable colleges. Fourteen years of age is too young to have the door of opportunity slammed in one's face because of parental carelessness or neglect. It's not up to the school; it's up to you.

Be sure, also, to check your son or daughter's confidential file at high school at the end of each year to be certain the record is "clean," by exercising your rights under the Federal Family Educational Rights and Privacy Act of 1974. Often called the "Buckley Amendment," the act was designed to prevent a childhood error in, say, seventh grade, from influencing your child's record throughout his or her school career. The school *must*, by federal law, give you access to such records. You have the right to examine even the most confidential school records concerning your child and to insist that mistakes of the past that might be a blot on an otherwise perfect record be removed after an appropriate period of time has passed. By insisting on seeing those files early in your child's high school career, you'll make teachers more hesitant to insert defamatory material in his or her folder.

Parents can also help their children fill in the endless forms and applications for various entrance examinations, and scholarship tests and applications: the SATs, ACTs, APs, financial aid applications, etc. Yes, it's important that young people learn to fill in such forms by themselves, but the number involved in the college application process is huge. And they are all so repetitive that filling them in accomplishes nothing after a while, except to deprive students of precious study time.

Parents can also help by driving their children to colleges for visits and interviews, to test sites for admissions exams, to and from school when work pressures become so great that students need the time that would be lost on long school bus rides for studying or handling college admissions applications.

Until the application process is completely computerized and automated, a parent who can type or use a word processor can be particularly helpful by editing and typing (not composing or originating) drafts of letters and college application forms. Typing these is an incredibly long process even for a skilled typist—and a difficult task for a less-than-skilled adolescent already burdened by a full load of daily homework, activities, and other chores at school and home.

Finally, helpful parents should also read as carefully as possible about prospective colleges and universities, so that they can share personal reactions with their children. It's rare that two people interpret anything the same way, and an adult's interpretation of complex material can often give a student new insights that can affect the decision-making process.

Obviously, there is little a parent can do to help if, as in too many families, your home is a battleground for ongoing parent-adolescent warfare. In many families, parents cannot or will not help. In other families, students won't let their parents help. Somehow, parent and student must find a way to end that war and join forces to face the outside world together if the college admissions process is to proceed successfully.

Indeed, I'm afraid that, without close parent-student cooperation, it may prove impossible to fulfill the promise of this book—to help any motivated student gain admission to the best possible college or university.

APPENDIX A
TIMETABLE FOR COLLEGE
ADMISSIONS PROCESS*

Freshman Year
(high school)

1.   Obtain software or directories of colleges such as *Barron's Profiles of American Colleges,* Cass and Birnbaum's *Comparative Guide to American Colleges, The College Board's Handbook, Peterson's Guide to Four-Year Colleges.* Select preliminary list of colleges that might eventually interest you.

2.   Select high school curriculum to meet requirements of colleges on preliminary list.

3.   Get to know your guidance counselor.

---

* This checklist represents the *ideal* timetable by which to follow the steps for getting into college. But don't worry if you are not a freshman or sophomore when you begin the process. The important thing is to *follow each step*—even if you're a senior. The further along you are when you begin the process, the less time you'll have to work with. To save time, I suggest that you telephone instead of write, and combine your college tours and interviews in the same visit.

Sophomore Year

Autumn:

Review and revise high school curriculum to meet requirements of colleges on preliminary list.

Spring:

1.   Enroll in AP courses for junior year if possible.

2.   Get to know your guidance counselor better.

Junior Year

Autumn:

1.   Sign up for PSATs.

2.   Obtain up-to-date college directories or software. Review and revise list of colleges that interest you. Copy profiles of each from *College Admissions Data Handbook* or obtain printouts from software.

3.   Write to all colleges on preliminary list for viewbooks, brochures, course catalogs, profiles and other materials of interest, including financial aid information. Data may also be available on computer software.

4.   Set up filing system, with individual folders for each college's correspondence and printed materials.

5.   Begin narrowing list of colleges to those of greatest interest, according to your own academic, artistic, athletic, social and environmental needs.

6.   Really get to know your guidance counselor—well!

Winter:

1.   Write or call colleges for schedule of campus tours during your winter and spring vacation periods.

2. Plan "circle tour" of all colleges on your list. Make necessary hotel and transport reservations.

3. Obtain schedules and forms for SAT I and Sat II tests, AP tests, from Educational Testing Service or high school guidance office. Mail immediately, with fees.

Spring

1. Campus tours. Obtain practice application forms. Make certain you're on mailing lists to receive all correspondence and applications, including financial aid forms, if appropriate. Inquire about personal interviews; set up appointments if possible.

2. Reduce number of colleges that interest you to between eight and 12.

3. Two weeks before beginning of first personal interviews, call or write for early-summer appointments.

4. Take SAT I and SAT II tests on appropriate dates.

5. Take AP tests on appropriate dates.

Spring-Summer:

1. Report to each college for personal interviews.

2. Send thank-you letter to each interviewer.

3. Narrow list of colleges to final four to eight.

Summer:

1. Fill out rough drafts of each college application.

2. Compose and type essays.

3. Type final application forms, deciding whether to apply for early decision or not.

4.   Send applications prior to or shortly after beginning of school year.

Senior Year

Autumn:

1.   Give recommendation forms to appropriate teachers, with stamped, self-addressed envelopes for returning them to colleges. Make certain forms are filled in at top with your name, address, school name, etc.

2.   Give School Report forms to proper school office. Fill in tops with your name, address, etc.

3.   Obtain autumn SAT I and SAT II test forms and mail to College Entrance Examination Board with fees—immediately.

4.   Sept. 15: Check with each teacher and with school office for status of all early-decision application forms.

5.   Nov. 1: Check with each teacher and with school office for status of all forms.

6.   Take SATs on appropriate dates.

7.   Oct. 1—Nov. 1: All early-decision applications due.

Winter:

1.   Dec. 1–31: Early-decision replies due.

2.   Jan. 1–Feb. 15: All college application and financial aid forms due.

3.   Final semester grades due at colleges when available.

Winter-Spring:

1.   Jan. 15–Apr. 15: Final acceptances, rejections due from each college.

2.   May 1–30: Deposits (nonrefundable) due on freshman tuition. Inform other colleges of your decision not to attend.

APPENDIX B
CHECKLIST FOR
COLLEGE ADMISSIONS
PROCESS

	College A	College B	College C	College D
Viewbook requested/received	....	....	....	....
Campus tour date	....	....	....	....
Personal interview date	....	....	....	....
Thank-you letter sent	....	....	....	....
Application requested/received	....	....	....	....
Essays completed	....	....	....	....
Application sent (certif. mail; rtn. recpt.)	....	....	....	....
Financial aid form sent	....	....	....	....
Recommendation forms given on [date] to Teacher A	....	....	....	....
Teacher B	....	....	....	....
School forms to office on	....	....	....	....
Final grade report forms	....	....	....	....

College Entrance Exams   - Dates
PSAT date & scores   Combined_____   Verbal_____   Math_____
SAT I date & scores   Combined_____   Verbal_____   Math_____
SAT I date & scores   Combined_____   Verbal_____   Math_____

SAT II dates, scores   AP test dates, scores

   Subject A_____   Subject A_____
   Subject B_____   Subject B_____
   Subject C_____   Subject C_____
                                   Subject D_____

APPENDIX C
SAMPLE COLLEGE
APPLICATION ESSAYS

Here is a collection of essays and excerpts of essays from some recent college applications. They range from wonderful to terrible. More often than not, the best writers tended to earn acceptances, while the worst found themselves rejected. In some cases, though, a fine writer found himself rejected because of poor high school grades. His writing, in other words, indicated a great deal of unrealized potential. As for mediocre writers, well, some were accepted, some rejected and some wait-listed. In effect, their writing was so average that it had little effect on their applications, which were then judged on other elements of their "packages"—high school grades, SAT I and SAT II scores, extracurricular activities, performance in the interview, etc. It is unimportant which of the writers whose essays you'll read were accepted or rejected. What is important is to examine the quality of the writing (how much effort did each writer put into the essay, do you think?), the originality, and what it tells you about the writer's personality. Although I've deleted the names, the essays or parts thereof (I've condensed some of them or merely reprinted excerpts) are as they appeared in each student's application—including misspellings, grammatical errors and errors in punctuation.

Evaluate a significant experience or achievement that has special meaning to you.

One more descent past the judges and a wave of the hand would signal me in or out. Most of us who were left now had equal skills. Some had more. Fewer than half of us would make it. To get that wave of acceptance I'd have to give it all I had—all stops out—no holding back—think positive—you'll make it—you WILL make it.

As I waited my turn to descend, my mind wandered back to what had brought me here. It had only been a few weeks earlier, when I was still 15, that a friend had asked if I had ever thought of being a ski instructor. He had been teaching for a year, enjoyed it, and thought I might too. A day later, I went to a meeting expecting to find 20 or 30 other interested young skiers. Instead, 200 showed up, and the next few weeks were spent on the slopes in ski clinics learning new skills and teaching techniques to apply to various age groups. It also was a time for the school instructors to observe their students and eliminate those they felt unqualified. I made the first cut.

Finally, all the clinics were over, and the supervisors were ready to give us our final test. We began by demonstrating fundamental techniques and slowly moved up the skill ladder until we were demonstrating our maximum skiing abilities. We had to ski past our classmates and 14 judges. It was one of the hardest things I'd ever done. I was scared spitless. Fear is funny. It makes you feel defeated before you start—shaky, rattled mentally, and sick to the stomach. I tried an old trick my Dad taught me: "Think of the worst possible thing that could happen, calculate the odds of that happening, make a decision, then whatever you decide stick with it and give it your best effort."

For me, the worst possible thing was making a fool of myself, racing down the hill, vomit spewing from my mouth, and winding up in a wipe-out at the spectators' feet. But suddenly I was off, dry mouth, sweaty palms, and all . . .

Now, as I put my ski pass around my neck, over my Ski Instructor's jacket, toss my skis in the truck and head for the mountains, it's hard to recall those moments of anxiety and uncertainty. I'm glad I hung in there. Hanging in there may not always win you the prize you seek, but it will always take you farther up the road.

Note: Here is an example of excellent writing. In addition to writing skills, though, this student's essay also displays his maturity through his insights into his emotions and the description of how he was able to set a difficult goal and achieve it through hard work and perseverance.

Please write and submit an essay on a subject of your choosing. Our aim is to learn more about you and to have a sample of your writing.

I am inter-racial—both black and white, or, depending on one's point of view, neither black nor white. Being inter-racial is different from being black or white. It produces special experiences and problems that are often difficult, often sad, often exciting and rewarding, but always enriching, because one learns the best and worst of many different worlds.

Last spring, for example, I saw the worst of one world when I shopped with my girl friend, who lives in an all-white neighborhood in the city, surrounded by minority slums with a high crime rate. As we waited in the check-out line, I noticed a white teenager fingering packs of chewing gum on the rack. The store manager watched him carefully, but said nothing. While the cashier rang my girl friend's purchases, I looked at the same gum rack, but touched nothing. Yet, as we started toward the door, the store manager ran forward and blocked our path.

"Buy what you take," he shouted, and then demanded that I turn open all my pockets. He made it clear that, solely because of my dark skin color, he suspected me of having stolen some chewing gum. He assumed that all dark-skinned people are naturally prone to steal. He could not understand that individuals steal, not whole races.

That was not my first experience with discrimination. Ironically, the first time was with black people who considered me too white—in the black slum, where I was born, the youngest of seven children. My parents abandoned us when I was 18 months old. We were scattered into various foster homes and have never seen each other since.

By the time I was six, I had lived in three foster homes, all in the ghetto. I vividly remember my last foster home, where I spent two years. Our house was dirty and run-down, full of rats and cockroaches. But those are not my worst memories.

When I was five, I entered kindergarten, where all the other children were black. My skin was tan and my hair straight and soft. In other words, I looked too white to be black, and the other children teased me, pulled my hair, and often hurt me.

When I was six, my black foster parents decided I was too white for them to adopt, and I was about to be institutionalized as a hard-to-place child when the State Bureau of Children's Services received an application from a white family to adopt a son—regardless of age or race.

Toward the end of that summer, a social worker came to my foster home and asked me to meet them and visit their home. A week later, I moved from the utter poverty of the black city slums to the wealth of the all-white suburbs. My new home looked like a park to me, with two landscaped acres, a swimming pool, tennis court, every imaginable game and toy, and a clean room of my own. I enrolled in the local elementary school.

Unfortunately, the racial discrimination I thought I had left behind in the city followed me to the suburbs, where now the rich white children found me too black to be white. So again, I was teased, hit, even spat upon during my first year at school. To make matters worse, there were other obstacles I had to get over. When I entered my new life, I could not read, write, or even speak properly. My speech and accent were that of a poor black child from the slums. I remember my first day of First Grade. I was the only child who was unable to follow the teacher's instructions to write out initials on a piece of paper. I didn't know what initials were or what the word meant, much less how to write them.

But with the guidance and love of my parents and teachers, I gradually learned to read and write. By the Third Grade, I had grown emotionally, intellectually, and socially enough to keep up with everybody else. From the poorest student in the First Grade, I had now reached "average" for my age and class.

Since then, everything has been uphill for me. By the end of Eighth Grade, my parents and I felt it was time for me to enroll in a superior high school. Although I started out slowly, by last spring, at the end of my junior year at [a prestigious, highly ranked high school], I was able to finish with a high honors average, among the top students in my class —and score a 4 in the AP European History examination. I am now confident I can do superior work at a demanding college like [name of school].

I feel my life has been an exciting one, filled with personal challenges and the satisfaction of meeting them. The challenge has often been to prove to myself that I could reach goals others said were too difficult or even impossible. Reading and writing seemed an impossible challenge in First Grade. High honors seemed beyond my reach when I entered Ninth Grade. J.V. tennis, working each summer, and scholarship itself —the research and accumulation of knowledge—have all been tremendously exciting and satisfying challenges.

But I think the experience that has proved the most important—and one that I am truly grateful I had—was to have lived in poverty as a young child. Most of my friends have lived in comfort all their lives, with most things handed to them. They take many of their advantages for granted. I feel this has hurt many of them. Most do not know in the slightest what it is like to be poor. Many are even unaware that poverty exists in America. Those that do know believe that the impoverished are simply lazy and refuse to work. Or, like the store manager I met in the city with my girl friend, they believe that dark-skinned people would rather steal than work.

I don't feel that way at all. I know how frustrating it is to be poor and uneducated, and this has made my mind more open. The experience of my first six years will guide me the rest of my life. I have returned several times with my father to see where I once lived in the city ghetto, and I know I will be active and do all I can to help children now in the same place I was. My experience also made me realize how important adoption is. There are so many children already alive who need the chance I had. I will never forget those years, and this will make my life all the better.

Note: Again, a fine example of good writing, combined with the ability and courage to set goals and achieve them through perseverance and hard work. His ability to overcome adversity, his lack of bitterness, his academic motivation, and his determination to convert his experience into a community contribution are all factors that influenced admissions committee members.

Evaluate a significant experience or achievement that has special meaning for you.

The two events in which I have been most involved, and, concurrently, have influenced me the most are my trip to France and my appointment as Editor-in-chief of the yearbook. The combination of those two rare opportunities has changed my life more drastically than any other occurence.

France is the most incredible place I have ever seen. That so much beauty and splendor could be concentrated in so small an area still amazes me . . . I know now there is much to be learned about the world; in the past, present, and the future.

More importantly, I learned about people. In a very brief time . . . I learned . . . that no matter what differences appear on the surface, people are intrinsically the same.

Soon after returning, I was notified of my appointment as yearbook editor. With this job came the largest responsibility I have as yet had to face.

I now realize that with this constant responsibility and obligatory dedication, I have become more disciplined . . . I find myself budgeting my time more wisely.

Through these two experiences, I feel I have profited enormously. I think I have developed more fully, both in my work and as a person.

Note: How many things are wrong with just the opening paragraph of this essay?   1. The question calls for *a* significant experience; the writer gives two!   2. The two opportunities are hardly apt to be "rare" among students applying to the highest-ranked American colleges.   3. Misuse of the word *drastically*, which means "severely," "suddenly" or "violently."   4. Sloppiness in his failure to retype this essay after correcting the misspelling in *drastically*. That failure is evidence that he lacks the very discipline he claims to have later on in his essay.   5. Misspelling of the word *occurrence*.

Evaluate a significant experience or achievement that has special meaning for you.

The automatic doors open and I enter the building. They close behind me while a I descend the stairs. As I near the bottom, a certain warmth seems to come over me. Feeling proud about what I am about to do, I proceed anxiously down the hall towards my destination: the special world of the pre-school unit of the rehabilitation ward at County General hospital.

Note: don't be melodramatic. Unless you're a particularly gifted writer with special talents, just tell your story in simple words—as the next applicant has done.

Evaluate a significant experience or achievement that has special meaning to you.

In February of my junior year, I took a week off from school to participate in a work camp in the heart of the city. It was arranged by a church fellowship program of which I am a member. This trip combined a number of different work experiences in a program that helped us to better understand the inner city. My main involvement was with a mobile soup kitchen. Our group consisted of twenty-four [high school] students and four adult advisors.

I remember one small man I met [at the soup kitchen] who spoke no English. He was dressed in a shabby three-piece suit with a number of patches. He also wore a shiny new pair of loafers, which seemed totally out of place on his feet. He came up to the girl next to me and tried to communicate. I tried to help out, but neither of us spoke Spanish, so we could not understand him. He gave us a big smile for our efforts, then jumped onto a small pedestal on the street corner and happily talked to the other street people. He opened my eyes to the fact that the street people were not . . . devoid of personality, but warm human beings. He had not been able to speak with us, but we were in fact able to communicate through a smile.

The trip helped me to grow and mature. I learned that no matter who or what a person appears to be, it is always wise to pay attention to what he or she has to say. Also, it taught me to avoid snap judgments about people because of their appearance. The experience was rewarding as well as fun [and it] made me feel good to help other people. I plan to go on a similar work camp in Philadelphia next spring vacation.

Note: Not great writing, but straightforward, simple, well organized, neat, warm, honest, with perfect grammar and spelling.

If you could travel through time and interview any historical figure, whom would you choose, what would you ask, and why?

One of the many names which come to my mind when thinking about this essay, the one that stood out most prominently was that of Louis XIV, the French king. Louis was the head of one of the most opulent courts in history. He built the indescribable palace of Versailles and was a shrewd and intelligent ruler.

If I had the chance to meet this man for an evening, there are many things would be many things I should like to ask and talk to him about . . .

> I would tell him of the democratic system in the United States . . .
> I want to know about the music and theater, who were Louis
> favorite musicians and performers, who composed his favorite
> music . . .

Note: I won't continue this essay. Sloppiness (. . . are many things
would be many things . . .), and grammatical and spelling errors
will mean automatic rejection at most colleges. The degree of
scholarship is quite low as well. In contrast, take a look at the next
essay answering the same kind of question.

*You are a journalist with the rare opportunity to interview any person
living, deceased or fictional. Whom would you choose? What questions
would you ask and why? What is the most important lesson you feel you
could learn from this person?*

> American journalist, editor, and author Walter Lippmann (b.
> 1889; d. 1974) was considered the dean of American journalists.
> His career spanned six decades and two world wars. Because my
> greatest academic interest is 20th century history, Lippmann
> would be the person I would most like to interview. He was not
> only one of the greatest observers of mankind's most remarkable
> century, he actually shaped the course of some of that history.
>
> An advisor to several presidents, he was a Wilson appointee to
> the American Commission to negotiate peace, in Paris, in 1917, and
> he was a frequent, though unofficial advisor to President Kennedy
> in 1962, in the days before the Cuban missile crisis.
>
> But he earned his greatest fame as a journalist. He wrote on
> virtually every important topic and interviewed almost every
> major historical figure during his 60 years as author and
> columnist. He covered the Progressive Movement of Theodore
> Roosevelt and the Watergate Scandal of Richard Nixon. He
> interviewed Wilson, Hoover, Roosevelt, Eisenhower, Churchill,
> Kennedy, Khrushchev, and many other world leaders. He won
> two Pulitzer Prizes, a Presidential Medal, and numerous other
> awards for his 25 books and thousands of newspaper and
> magazine columns and articles.
>
> I think Lippmann understood better than any other
> commentator of his day why one event led to and fed off other
> events. I think an interview with him could teach me what he
> believed were the crucial political errors of the years he covered
> world events.

I would ask Lippmann how he believes those errors changed the course of history, how they might have been avoided, and how things might have worked out had they been avoided. More specifically, I would ask him the following questions as well:

1. Do you think the Progressive Movement of the early 20th Century produced real political, social, and industrial reform or was it just a political ploy to win elections?

2. Did Franklin D. Roosevelt's programs to end the Depression create greater problems than they were supposed to solve—both at the time and in the future?

3. What measures do you think could have been taken in the 1930's to prevent Hitler's military build-up?

4. How big a role did journalism play in escalating the Cold War?

5. Why did the U.S. not learn before it entered the Vietnam War what the French had learned after their defeat?

I think the lesson to be learned from answers to questions like these from a man like Lippmann would be how today's leaders could change the course of future events by not repeating the errors of the past.

Evaluate a significant experience or achievement that has special meaning for you.

He was gripping his chest in pain, and on his pale face was the expression of desperation. He was crouched down on his knees between first and second base, leaning his whole body back and forth. Finally he collapsed and lay still on the ground. And before I realized it he was dead.

It was one of those typical hot, humid summer Sundays, I was playing softball with the local adult league, but it was one that I will never forget. The man's name was Sal. He was forty-eight years old, married, with three children. The cause of his death was a heart attack, but this was not his first, he had had some other heart trouble in the past. Sal was playing softball against the doctor's orders, but those who knew him well said that he liked the game too much to obey them . . .

I never really knew Sal, yet he still has had an effect upon me. Over the past few years I have learned what type of person he was. He was a man who was able to tell himself what he wanted in his life, and what elements enhanced it. Heart trouble did not stop Sal from playing softball. The game made him happy even though he knew what consequences it could bring. He was a person who believed that the best thing to do, in a situation or decision, results in individual happiness.

Note: The essay is certainly warm, honest, etc., and starts off pretty well. But his grammar and spelling deteriorate, and the meaning of his last sentence is unintelligible.

There are limitations to what grades, scores, and recommendations can tell us about any candidate. Please use the space on the back of this page to let us know something about you that we might not learn from the rest of your application.

It is very difficult to describe oneself, but in preparing this application I have tried to be as objective as possible.

I am very outgoing. Recently, I received the lead in my high school play. I have also been in other productions. Being involved with drama has also given me good communications skills.

I realized that early in my high school career I was an under-achiever, but I am now on the right track.

I enjoy sports as a spectator, but was never very good as a participant. I do wish I had participated more ...

I know that [name of college] would be a good place for me. The location and physical environment alone are enough to encourage anyone to apply. I also like the fact that it is a small school, yet I don't feel that I would miss out on anything because [name of college] offers such a wide variety of courses and activities. I was also impressed with the intimacy and friendliness of [name of college]. I very much want to become a [name of college] student.

Note: Don't use the essay or interview to discuss psychological problems; don't "preach to the converted" by telling school officials what they already know—that it's a small school (they want to know why you want to go to a small school); and don't beg! The next writer makes the same error by overexposing psychological problems without showing how they contributed to a better understanding of humanity or family life, or how the experience was truly significant.

Evaluate a significant experience or achievement that has special meaning to you.

About two years ago my parents decided to get a divorce. This breakup was difficult for me to live with at first but now I am very happy along with my two brothers aged fifteen and eleven. This experience has been very influential in my life. It has shown me the importance of a family and togetherness.

My parents had been very happy until a few years ago. Every once in a while they would get into an argument that would wake me up. They would tell me not to worry about it and that they loved each other too much to ever think of getting a divorce. After about a couple of years of my dad living in the city where his business was and seeing him on weekends, I was told that they were going to be separated for a while. The news was a shock but I accepted it in a reasonable amount of time.

Both of my parents were recently married. They seem very happy now and my brothers and I are happy for them. But their period of separation held some difficulties for us. I gained some insight as to what a serious commitment involved. I also learned how difficult it can be to try to maintain a marriage while raising a family at the same time. For a relationship to work there must be agreements and sacrifices made.

Note: Your own essay must show more depth and far better punctuation for your application to receive serious consideration.

Evaluate a significant experience or achievement that has special meaning to you.

"Miss Gordon will see you now."

It was the first of many times that I was to be summoned by the millionaire doyenne of Off-Broadway Theater. Owner of her own theater in New York and in the Country Playhouse in New England, Miss Gordon knew them all—actors, playwrights, and presidents. The dimly lit study was supportive of a beauty who had debuted in silent movies. Suddenly this contemporary of Mary Pickford was speaking to me.

"No school drama experience, dear?" I lamely agreed that my interest in the theater was, at the very best, latent. I saw the job slipping away from me. We chatted.

"The purpose of the Country Playhouse is to act as a showcase for new works by both established and new authors. A new play premiers each week for twelve weeks." Finally, the tiny, breathy voice got to the point. "You are hired, Elizabeth. Welcome to the world of the theater."

Like Alice in Wonderland, I was in strange territory. It was to be a summer of building confidence through knowledge and maturity. I soon began to appreciate the need for consistency, concentration, and focus. I learned the value of inspiration and humility. I did not know it, but that day held a sign-post for me saying, "This way for a *new* you."

I hammered, painted, and sawed my way through the summer. Working space was often cramped and hot; anxiety was a silent partner. Would we finish by opening night? As my manual skills increased, so did my desire to use them creatively outside the theater. A freshly painted bedroom and request for power tools for Christmas shocked my parents.

If my manual dexterity inched along, my social skills took a quantum leap. How could I let shyness hamper the greeting . . . of V.I.P.'s—Broadway producers up for a look?

As the mid-summer mark passed, I noticed my appearance was different. I lost weight, thanks to a combination of perpetual motion and a brown rice regimen introduced by a dance troupe. I [soon] seemed to be more in charge of me.

The amount of "scut" work jobs abounds in all theaters. Flyers must be circulated, props have to be sorted, repainted, and stored, and even bathrooms need to be scrubbed. Less manual, but equally lacking in creativity, were tasks such as ordering rehearsal night dinners from local chicken take-out places, arranging for flowers for stars, pressing costumes, and ushering. These menial tasks earned my disdain until I overheard a chance remark by a director: "There are no minor roles, just minor players."

There were weekly tests of my ability to juggle several tasks at once and to remain cool in a crisis. I wanted to earn the approval of my cohorts. Laundering and then drying—with a hair dryer—a star's dress during a ten minute intermission got me a standing ovation from our crew. One opening night found the entire crew incapacitated. Could I substitute? I could and did. The play will open at an Off Broadway theater in the spring.

So ended the summer. A mini-course in theater production or a rehearsal for life?

Note: This is wonderful writing, and the story displays enormous maturity. As in the first two essays, this student shows motivation, courage, and ability to set difficult goals and achieve them. These are the characteristics every college seeks in the students it accepts.

APPENDIX D
COLLEGE ENTRANCE
EXAMINATIONS (PSAT, SAT I,
SAT II, ACT):
AN EXPLANATION

Most college entrance examinations for American colleges and universities are sponsored either by the College Entrance Examination Board (CEEB) or the American College Testing Program. The CEEB examinations are administered by the Educational Testing Service (ETS) of Princeton, New Jersey. ETS administers three sets of exams, the first of which is a two-hour practice test in the autumn of the junior year of high school.

PSAT

The Preliminary Scholastic Assessment Test (PSAT) is a first exam that gives students across America what may be their initial experience in quick thinking. Divided into a one-hour verbal and one-hour mathematics section, the PSAT asks dozens of questions that demand instant responses from a choice of four or five answers listed beside each question.

ETS does not send PSAT scores to any colleges. They are sent to each student and to his high school guidance counselor or college adviser as a guide for college selection. ETS believes that PSAT scores are a good indication of how each student will fare on SATs; and many high schools tend to steer students with low PSAT scores to less-competitive colleges.

I believe that can often be a serious error, because under certain circumstances, many of America's most competitive colleges often excuse low SAT scores (and, therefore, PSAT scores) in evaluating many applicants. So, the most realistic approach to PSATs is simply to relax and take them for what they are—a *practice* test that counts for practically nothing in the college admissions process. No one will see them but you and your guidance counselor, and regardless of how disappointing the results may be, don't let low scores or your guidance counselor dissuade you from applying to a top college if you firmly believe you have enough positive attributes to outweigh the effects of low PSAT or SAT scores.

There are a couple of other things to keep in mind about PSATs. One is that they can, if you choose, serve as the first step in the national competition for National Merit Scholarships (see p. 000). In that case, your PSAT scores will count for something—but only if you do well, not if you do poorly. Obviously, winning a National Merit Scholarship will be one more positive element in your admissions package.

PSAT scores also serve to trigger a nationwide search by colleges for candidates whose scores and student profiles most match the kinds of applicants they seek. So, depending on your PSAT performance and profile, you'll automatically receive mailings from colleges encouraging you to apply.

Another thing to keep in mind is that PSAT scores do indeed correlate with SAT I scores. So, if your PSAT scores are low, you may want to start getting some tutoring to improve your ability to handle such tests. At least buy some of the many available books with practice SAT I and II tests and get busy practicing.

SAT I

In the spring of your junior year you'll take the first of two batteries of ETS exams. You're only required to take them once, however, and if you do well enough the first time—a combined score of 1550 or better, for example—by all means skip them the second time, unless you think you can improve on such scores.

The SAT I lasts two and one-half hours and consist of two parts: Verbal Reasoning and Mathematical Reasoning. Each part has three sections lasting about 30 minutes, 30 minutes and 15 minutes, respectively. Each part is scored on a scale of 200 to 800, with 1600 equaling a perfect combined score for the two parts.

The system of scoring SATs, in effect since the beginning of 1995, grades on a curve that automatically makes a score of 500 in each part, or a combined score of 1000, the *average* score each year for all students. So, if you score above 500 on either the verbal or math SAT, your score is above average for the nation.

Median scores of students admitted to the four dozen most competitive colleges in *Barron's*, however, are well above average, ranging around 625, while the median for students admitted to the second most competitive group is about 615. Remember, however, that median means *middle*. In other words, half the students admitted to the most selective colleges had scores below the median figure.

The Verbal Reasoning sections are made up of about 80 questions. Half are in the Reading Comprehension section that measures your ability to read and think critically, by asking you to read a lengthy passage with several points of view. It then asks questions that test your ability to write well, to interpret and reason logically and to arrive at correct conclusions. The other two sections consist of rapid-response objective questions. One section is made up of sentence completion questions; the other, analogies that test your vocabulary (e.g., expansion=contraction:enlargement= ?).

The Mathematical reasoning section of the SAT I consists of 35 multiple choice, 15 quantitative comparison and 10 student-produced response questions. Obviously, the first two groups are objective questions requiring speedy responses. The last group requires you to develop your own answers. You're permitted to take a calculator to the exam.

You may be tempted to guess the answers of many multiple choice questions. If they are "educated" guesses, by all means do so, but *don't*, whatever you do, take wild guesses, because you'll be penalized a fraction of a point for each wrong answer. Thus, three or four wrong guesses, depending on the penalty, will wipe out your score for each correct answer. To make educated guesses on a multiple choice question, eliminate the absurd possibilities, then see if you can determine the answer that seems most likely to be correct among the remaining choices.

Like every test you've ever taken, there will be some easy and some difficult questions. Scan the test quickly and answer the easy ones immediately to score as many easy points as you can right away. You get as many points for questions that take you 10 seconds to answer as you do for those that take 10 minutes. So answer the easy ones first. But be careful to enter each answer into the appropriate box for that question. If you answer questions out of order, as I suggest, watch the numbers of each question and answer box *carefully*, to avoid putting the *right* answer in the *wrong* box!

You can take SATs as often as you like. They're offered six or seven times a year, depending on the state. All your scores are reported to the colleges, although they only consider the two highest in judging your application. It's inadvisable though, to take them more than twice—first, because of the added stress it will place on you in an already stressful year; and, second, because scores seldom vary much without extensive tutoring. Most students take SAT Is in the spring of their junior year, take some tutoring over the summer months, then repeat them in the fall of their senior year.

SAT II

The other battery of tests you may have to take for admission to some colleges are the SAT II subject tests. Once known as Achievement Tests, they consist of one-hour, short-answer examinations in any of a dozen or more subjects, including English composition, literature, American history, European history, mathematics, biology, chemistry, physics and a number of foreign languages. The majority of the most selective colleges require three SAT II tests, but some only require one test (usually English composition) and a few require none at all. Some specify the tests you *must* take; others let you choose your own.

Some colleges that place a little less emphasis on the SAT I use the SAT II tests as the equivalent of admissions tests, because they feel the SAT IIs are true measures of the academic knowledge you've acquired during your high school years. Many colleges also use the SAT II tests as placement examinations to determine whether to let you skip a freshman college requirement in a particular subject and allow you to jump right into advanced work.

Some colleges will give you course credits for the freshman courses you're allowed to skip. So, if you're particularly strong in one or more academic areas, by all means take the SAT IIs in those subjects to display your strengths—even if the college doesn't require any SAT IIs. Be sure to check whether the colleges you apply to will give you course credits for high school SAT II test scores. That's like money in the bank, because you'll be able to finish college sooner if you want to and thus save a portion of your costs of tuition, room and board.

Remember, too, that grades and GPAs vary from high school to high school and have different values, depending on the ranking of your school. SAT II tests are national standards that measure everyone alike. SAT IIs are true measures of your academic strengths, and they can often offset the effects of low scores on your SAT I.

One tip, though: Take the SAT II tests in your strong subjects at the end of the last year in which you will be studying that subject. Remember: You can take the tests anytime—even at the end of your freshman or sophomore year. So, if you've finished your school's advanced biology course at the end of sophomore year, for example, and you've done exceptionally well, take the SAT II then, while the material is still fresh in your mind. Don't wait until the end of your junior year or the beginning of your senior year, and then have to restudy all the material from scratch to prepare for the test.

And here's another tip: You can take *as many SAT II tests as you want!* In other words, you can take one in every subject you study, save up the scores and then select the best three scores to send to the colleges to which you apply. So, if you're not sure which subject areas you'll do best in, take SAT II tests in all of them! (You can only take three tests on one given test date, however.)

Most high schools have the application forms for taking PSATs and SATs, along with lists of test sites. It's up to you to get the forms on time, fill them out and mail them with the appropriate fees to College Entrance Examination Board Service, Box 6200, Princeton, NJ 08541; or Box 1025, Berkeley, CA 94701, if you live in the West. If your school does not have the proper forms, write to or call The College Board immediately. Once you've sent in your forms and the proper fees, they'll send you tickets, which you will need to enter the test rooms. Don't misplace them. You will not be admitted to the test sites without them. In your organizational file, keep a special folder for SAT I and SAT II test materials.

ACT

The American College Testing Program (P.O. Box 414, Iowa City, IA 52240) has an alternative battery of college entrance examinations (the ACTs) lasting three hours. Widely accepted in the West and Midwest, they are accepted somewhat less frequently by Eastern colleges as substitutes for SATs.

Unlike the SATs, ACTs are a single battery of four tests: English, mathematics, reading and science reasoning, taking 45, 60, 35 and 35 minutes, respectively, or a total of about three hours. The four test scores are averaged to obtain a composite ACT score. Median scores of students admitted to the two most competitive groups of colleges listed in *Barron's* were 28 or higher.

The ACT English test has five passages to read. Each is followed by multiple choice questions—a total of 75 in all—that measure your punctuation, grammar, spelling, vocabulary and other English skills. Unlike SAT tests, there is *no penalty* for wrong answers. So, by all means, answer all questions, even if you take a wild guess. Only the correct answers will be counted. And work as fast as you possibly can. You've got to answer 75 questions in 45 minutes, or one answer every 36 seconds!

The ACT Mathematics Test has 60 questions—one a min-ute—in five areas: pre-algebra, elementary algebra, intermedi-ate algebra, plane geometry and trigonometry. Again, as in all the ACT tests, you won't be penalized for wrong answers. So answer every question—even if you have to guess.

The ACT Reading Test has 40 questions measuring reading comprehension. Half the questions deal with social studies and science and half with prose fiction and the humanities.

The ACT Science Reasoning Test deals with your basic knowledge of biology, chemistry, physics, geology and astron-omy. It gives you seven sets of data to evaluate and asks 40 questions that test your reasoning skills rather than your spe-cific knowledge of any of the sciences mentioned.

Studying in advance for the ACTs has proved far more effective than studying for SATs, because, like the CEEB SAT II subject tests, the ACTs are based more on actual knowledge obtained in the classroom. So by all means buy the various books with sample ACTs and tips on preparing for them.

INDEX

Special skills   63
Special students   27–28
Stafford Loans—*See Federal Stafford Loans*
State grants to college students 135–136
Student loans   138–142—*See also Loans*
Summer jobs   31, 49–50, 101, 134
Summer school   8
Supplemental Educational Opportunity Grants (SEOGs) 135

T

TAs—*See Teaching assistants*
Teacher recommendations   51–54, 103–104, 122, 123–124, 160
Tours of colleges   24–27, 72–90, 158–159
Teaching assistants   26–27, 30, 77
Transfers   151–152
Tuition payment plans   146–147

U

Unique qualities that make you special   52, 69–70, 83–86, 111–118
Unsolicited materials from colleges   21, 24
U.S. Department of Education 142–143

V

Videos   21, 30
Viewbooks   21–24, 34, 70, 158
Visiting college campuses   24–27, 72–90, 158–159

W

Wait-listing   150–151
"Well-rounded students," the myth of   3, 47–48
Wintergreen Orchard House, Inc. 19
Women's education   11–13
Work experience   31, 49–50, 101, 107, 134
Work-study programs   31, 49–50, 102, 107